1966

This book may be kept

FOURTEEN DAYS

A fine will be charged for each day the book is kept

ONE TOUCH OF FRANCE

BY A. HAMILTON GIBBS

Gun Fodder

Soundings · Labels · Bluebottles

Harness · Chances · Undertow

Rivers Glide On · The Need We Have

A Half Inch of Candle · Way of Life

One Touch of France

ONE TOUCH OF FRANCE

With decorations by

A. Hamilton Gibbs

Doubleday & Company, Inc., Garden City, N.Y., 1953

Library of Congress Catalog Card Number: 52-13558

DEDICATION

For an unforgettable year in your school, acquiring far more than the language, I thank you Saint-Malo.

For what you taught me in four years of mud, blood, horror and death from Mons to Compiègne, I thank you Northern France.

For the winter of rain, fog, dinge, in the Rue Cassette, I thank you Paris.

For a winter of sun, blue sea, friend-making, in the Boulevard Victor Hugo, I thank you Nice.

For three hard-working, writing-painting winters in an enchanted villa, I thank you Antibes.

For a novel written facing the delicious contours of the Cap, I thank you Golfe Juan.

For many games of golf on your rolling fairways, I thank you Mougins.

7

For the urge to write this present oddity after twelve long years of absence, I thank you Saint-Paul.

For revealing yourselves to me while I made daubs of you on canvas, I thank you all—Carros, Eze, Villefranche, Antibes, Mougins, Saint-Paul, Saint-Jeannet, Gilette, Sigale, Castellane, Biot, Cagnes, Villeneuve-lès-Avignon.

For the many times I have climbed the Escalier de Sainte Anne, with the fig tree growing out of the wall, I thank you Avignon.

For all the countless miles I have driven in your mountains and along your coastline from Italy to Spain, I thank you Provence.

For all your good food, good wine, good hours, I thank you innkeepers of France.

For all the kindness, the hospitality, the sympathy, the happiness, the inspiration that you have always given me, I thank you people of France.

PRELUDE

Why, in an English boy of thirteen, an instant leap of spirit on being asked if he would like to go to school in France?

Why, within a week at the Collège de Saint-Malo, the quick sloughing off of British self-consciousness, to find waiting underneath unexpected layers of warm receptivity, of sub-conscious recognition, of mutual understanding?

Why, in the next fifty years, in many meetings with the French abroad or at home on my many returnings to France, have these, all, remained in full flowering?

Perhaps an answer lies in that the Norman, Guilbert, left his seed behind after the Conquest and the Angles made the name Gibbs.

Perhaps there is something in the unclarified legend in the family of a French great-grandmother.

Perhaps if these two have truth, the emotional impact, the call, of Aucassin and Nicolette—read to me at the age of nine—was beyond my blood-resistance.

But whether or not I can lay it at the door of that hypothetical drop of thinned blood, either of female parent or of lusty Guilbert, is of the least importance.

For me what counts is that I was able to hear the tapping, to obey the inner command, to go out across the cloying Channel into a world made larger, whose people gave me of their sustenance, helped me to grow, rendered me incapable of forgetting.

SAINT-MALO

1. Then and Now

Perched on a pinpoint rock,
your ramparts in the pounding sea,
your cluttered roofs climbing like altar steps
to the upreaching spire of a grand cathedral,
you were perfection.
You were all the gathered past,
the finished present,
the assured future . . .
And today you lie gutted,
a shambles.

You received me when a small urchin,
alien,
not speaking your tongue,
ignorant of the ways of your thinking,
gaping at newness,
obstinate in the belief of a perfidious slogan:

that an Englishman could lick a Frog with one hand tied behind his back.

In disproving that
you taught me to unlearn other crass knowledge.
You taught me that unlearning, indeed, was the first step to
learning.

Straight from the softness of a parent's warm hands,
you showed me your hardness,
initiated me to cold—
the hardly bearable ice-cold of standing alone
among incomprehensible savages,
hearing the strange sound of snipping as apron strings were
cut.
The ensuing nakedness you took and breathed upon,
moulded in your Breton fingers,
shaped to the standard of your values,
clothed, finally, in the richness of your stern affection.

You gave me first your language,
disturbingly potent,
magnificently uprooting,
passkey to the door of imagination,
challenge to emerge from the snailshell of self,
stepping stone to discovery, forward and backward . . .
rich loam for a transplanting.

Then came important things,
unknown, unfelt till then:
love of old walled towns with winding cobbled streets uphill
and down;
smell of roasting coffee in the early morning;
terrific carillon of bells;
exciting perfume of ships' chandlers on an ancient dock;
lusty music of street vendors;
thrill of green waves breaking white on golden sand;
tingle of sea on naked body;
of hot sand between toes;

perfection of seagulls and swift precision of sandpipers;
delight of rocky pools draped with marvellous seaweed,
populous with shrimps marooned by the receding tide;
bewitchment of the names of far-off places—
Douarnenez, Madagascar, Hawaii, Samarkand . . .
the lasting itch to "be'old this world so wide."
These you gave me.

Perceptions,
of truth's strength,
of discipline that has to seep from within,
of the hard meaning of justice, and its opposite,
of friendship and its exigencies,
of grief and its cutting edge.
These, too, you gave me.

In your keeping the alien slip responded to Malouin grafting,
put down roots that have not withered,
that have spread through all the land of France,
that have brought me back and back again,
to renew, to add, to acknowledge,
and to give, however little, in return—
the terrifying years of endless days and nights from Mons to
    Armistice;
in older age the teaching of your language to new fighters in
    your new need;
and in between and all the time
the transmuting of your grafting to the daily task of living.

You were reality then
in all that you stood for,
in the justifiable pride of your centuries,
in the slow carving of your good way of life,
in your enviable men whose deeds are recorded in statuary,
in the italicised lines that you inscribed in the chronicle of
    world history.

You are reality today
in all that you stand for of terror, of brutality, of devastation.

Among the carefully piled rubble of what were once your
   quiet house of God,
your noisy Grand'Place,
your big streets and little, straight and winding,
your palaces and homes,
whether of corsair or "terreneuvier,"
of high or humble,
of woman or child—
among these the wind now makes weird empty music.

What, then, was it that destroyed you?
Guns were the mere instrument.
Against what, then, will your bastions now be patched,
your ramparts made secure,
the spire of your new cathedral reach once more to the sky?

What is there here for my unlearning?

2. The School

Bourné, Lapostolle, de Couesbouc, Toulou, de Courcelles . . .
names that come leaping out through the years,
faces that I see clearly,
not of today, like my own, carved deep,
but as we all were then,
growing and unknowing,
sturdy kids, apple-cheeked, blue-eyed, blond,
dark as Indians, and as lithe;
upper lips, some, already pencilled with hair—cramming phi-
    losophy and rhetoric—
chins, some, unscraped to coax the hesitant beard.
Sons of "terreneuviers"—those fishers of the Grand Banks—
    of lawyers, farmers, doctors, ships' captains,
sons of butcher, baker, candlestick maker,
coming from Saint-Malo's fortress town,
from Rennes and Cancale,
from Paramé and Saint Ideuc,

from Mont Saint Michel and Plougastel,
sons of all Brittany;
extern and intern, meaning day boy and boarder,
from babies of eight, conducted home each afternoon down
the cobbled hill,
to men of eighteen, ready for Bachaud and the outer world . . .
growing, and unknowing that in the space of a decade
we should all be digging trenches
from Belgium to Switzerland,
from Saloniki to the Dardanelles,
from Mesopotamia to Jerusalem.

But our beginning was the school and the school was good.
Hourly, cathedral bells flooded us with melody.
The salt of the encircling sea was always on our lips.
Our young learning encompassed more than written texts, in
little things and big:
the slow warming of ice-cold study rooms by collective heat
of restless bodies;
the secret manufacture of three-nibbed pens for speedier
copying of lines inflicted as punishment;
the swift successful trajectory of notes, one to another, by
means of rubber bands attached to first and second fingers;
the thrill of momentary escape by pretending an urgent need
of nature;
the science of speech without lip-motion during marchings
along corridors from one classroom to another;
the swapping of slang unfit for priestly ears in gravelled playground—place of all too brief freedom
for yelling, running, mauling, penny skittles, football;
place also for relieving ourselves in latrines of caveman simplicity,
waterless holes most odorful,
behind doors inscribed, illustrated, with schoolboy filth.

In the dormitory—
long rows of curtained cubicles—
we learned to rise, sticky-eyed, with the sun,

to simulate washing behind ears,
to show wet brush that had not touched teeth,
to fasten vital buttons on the run.

In the chapel,
tender-kneed on bare wooden planks,
we learned to time each priest
and bet rare sous on which would gallop fastest through his
    mass.

In the refectory,
vast hall for priests as well as boys,
we learned the rancidness of third day butter,
kept individually in drawers beneath the long tables;
learned to eat it just the same, on wedge-shaped slices of
    superb bread,
to wash it down in foaming bowls of chocolate,
or bitter cider,
according to the meal's hour.

For learning's climax: the solemn promenades,
Thursdays, Sundays too,
afternoons of mixed blessing,
in files of three, a hundred-legged crocodile;
so well behaved, at first,
down the enticing shopping street—joy always for eyes and
    ears—
out through the Grand'Porte to the glamorous quais;
then the long slog, discipline waning, to Paramé,
there to repose at last on golden sand
where, one day, the whole piled Atlantic would come tumbling
    in,
the next, steal whispering up the beach.
And there, innocent-seeming but wary-eyed,
while conducting priest was engaged with breviary,
we mastered the secret cupping of a cigarette behind the hand,
the invisible grown-up trickling of forbidden smoke through
    stinging nostrils.

Priests . . .
old and young,
pleasant, not so pleasant, unpleasant;
essential sheep dogs barking at young heels,
omnipresent through the day's twenty-four hours,
through our sleeping and our waking,
our working and our playing,
our eating and our praying.
What more natural than that, learning from them, we learned
  also them?
None could hide from our reaching eyes what lay under the
  soutane,
whether of good, of bad, of only indifferent.
Some, lay figures merely, throwing no shadow, emitting no
  light.
Some, all priest but no man, suffering not us little ones.
Some, combining wilful bite with sour bark, sadistic in au-
  thority; priests but not men of God;
nor even decent men;
commanding attention, but not holding respect.

Out from among them all stood three,
towering,
commanding nothing, but holding everything, attention, respect, affection too:
men,
not using the soutane as egocentric screen,
as hideout, covering weakness,
as insurance against the forces of hell,
but as work clothes for a chosen task.
Men, these three, first and always;
content, being themselves,
therefore quick in grasp and sympathy at others' gropings;
using laughter, unscared of tonsure, instead of the barbed
  verbal arrow,
discussion instead of tempery punishment,
cooperation instead of clerical rejection.
One was the Abbé Juhel,

fortyish, gone already at the knees, but uncaring,
awkward of hand and foot,
severe, hidden, remote behind far-off occupied eyes,
tightly self-girded to compete with the daily torture of small
    boys,
with the difficult maintenance of discipline,
with the redundant dinning of ABC's into thick heads,
with the continuous suffering of impertinent assault . . .
but coming out to us soon with the shy gentleness of lamb
    playing lion,
his roars off-key, unshaking,
betraying native wool beneath assumed mane.

Shrewd imps, we picked him as natural target for liliputian
    goading,
striving to evoke the lion;
and when our tiny arrows of misconduct pricked him to snap-
    ping point—
a roar of five hundred lines to the whole class—
clapping was the sign of our victory,
to Juhel's consternation,
bringing more applause,
and then . . . his slow twinkling smile
and his intentioned forgetting of the five hundred lines.
Vive Monsieur Juhel!

Second of these was Monsieur Percepied:
galvanising as a cold shower,
flames for eyes,
laughter always lurking, with and not at,
quick answer enticing us to laugh.
In the early thirties then,
straight, stocky, strapping, goodlooking,
at ease with himself,
with life,
with us.
Remove the soutane and there stood the defender of Bastogne,
the court lawyer,

the engineer,
the leader of any forlorn hope
demanding impact of brain, personality, drive,
to lift run-of-the-mill to final point of effort, and beyond.

If it be sin for priest to enjoy his own talent,
then was Monsieur Percepied sinner indeed;
taking frank pride in a Metropolitan baritone,
as full of challenging sex as Caruso's tenor;
his "Ave Maria," like the great Italian's, a passionate love song,
making rubble of chapel walls.

Sin?
Only the sadist could count it so
when he could give—as once to me, alone—for an enraptured
    hour,
the noble largesse of his voice.
Off bounds, he caught me, at a pedal organ in the priest's
    recreation room.
Others would have asked how I came there, and by whose
    permission.
Instead, listening to my musical fumblings,
he laughed, swept me from the organ bench, arm like a steel
    bar,
said: "So you like music, hein? Eh bien . . ."
And then, playing his own accompaniment,
the flow of proud liquid gold—arias, folksongs, ballads of the
    troubadours . . .
generous enchantment to a trespassing urchin . . .
not sinning, surely;
but rather, brother to the Juggler-Monk
who offered his tricks as prayer to the accepting Madonna.

Third of the triumvirate was Monsieur Meriais,
last because he stood first,
because he gave most,
because he has remained longest in an inner niche of the
    heart.

Officially, Monsieur l'Abbé Meriais;
affectionately, to us all, Père Jean.

I see again the storm-wrenched steamer that had brought me,
mercifully motionless at the dock under the high ramparts;
see myself, stomach emptied many times through the dread-
     ful night;
still empty, and knotted tight at strangeness;
see also, and forever, bearing down upon me,
a curiously dressed giant from this other planet,
huge of shoulders, of hands, of feet;
myself, barely chest-high to him, a scared pygmy.
Brick-red cheeks were covered with stubble like silver wire in
     the seven o'clock sun.
Pince-nez were clamped to a jutting nose.
Black skirts swished as he clumped along the deck,
head topped off with a shovel hat;
black bib bordered with white beads at his Adam's apple,
black cape swinging from a hairy hand.

This giant halted, looking down at me.
In English he said: "Hullo! You must be Arthur Gibbs. I'm
     Monsieur Meriais."
His enormous hand engulfed mine,
not making bones crack,
but gentle as St. Bernard offering paw.
Up there in his face occurred a strange melting process.
It was not carved out of red rock any more,
not when a smile cracked it,
not when you saw that the smile was in his eyes too.
Miraculously, the world was steady again.
You found that you were not scared any more,
that stomach muscles were unknotting,
that he was no longer giant, nor altogether priest,
but man,
the man to whom you could tell everything,
of whom ask anything,
the man you would follow anywhere . . .

And did,
through all the four seasons of that long French year;
through the streets of Saint-Malo, Saint-Servan, Paramé,
    Rothéneuf,
where every six paces his hat would be off
in response to his name, warmly, on the lips of friends;
followed along dusty country roads
where black and silver magpies were always a tree ahead;
into the homes of Breton farmers
whose eyes lit up at his coming,
who pulled out for him cider and biscuits and apples
and smiles and urgent talk;
followed along the digue to the lee of sheltering rocks,
there to undress, go crashing through the surf,
battered and tingling, into deep water;
followed, too, inevitably,
by asking, by listening, by this companionship,
into the still pool of his being,
clean,
unrippled,
inaccessible to anger, to any meanness, to the others' quick
    pathetic spite.

Ally always in the day's adventure,
sanctuary in moments of distress . . .
perhaps, subconsciously, one tries to follow him still, le bon
    Père Jean.

Thus, then, through autumn's mellow gorgeousness,
through the bitter gales of winter,
through the quick mending of spring's touch,
and on until the regretted end of summer's long magnificence,
I was one of you all,
indistinguishable,
blue-uniformed like the rest,
merged,
thinking in your terms,
sharing and enjoying your way of life,

no longer any "perfidious" Channel between the learning and
the understanding of each other.

At last, too soon, indelible, the day of another cutting;
the emotional bewilderment and upheaval of goodbyes;
wavings from the boat's deck,
in loneliness and shock of loss . . .
And then . . . England again,
strangely different to new eyes that now held comparison.

NORTHERN FRANCE

November 1914 . . . and back, strangely, to France,
not any more in the blue of Saint-Malo's preparatory school,
but in the King's khaki, prescribed for the new postgraduate
   course.
Grown now—there has been just time for that—but still unknowing;
our teachers already at the gates of Paris.
Bourné, Lapostolle, de Couesbouc, all the others, out there
   somewhere,
studying in the mud;
and I . . . still one of you; like you, a simple soldier,
about to learn, like you, old places tainted with new forms of
   death;
to learn, like you, the smell of fear's recurring decimal;
to learn, like you, the formulae of new equations,
old as time, but not taught in any other school . . .
the formulae, but never the elusive answer.

Four and a half years to the course,
a glimpse of Egypt and a touch of Greece thrown in,

but mostly back and forth across the tortured map of France,
belching incessant shrapnel from my battery of guns;
on two legs, mostly,
on a horse sometimes,
in a train once or twice;
through France's woods and fields and towns and villages,
on cobbles and dirt roads,
the feel of it soaking into one's bones;
its colors, noises, smells,
its look in snow, in rain, in revealing sun and shapeless night;
snatching sleep on its earth, and in the holes one dug into its
    earth;
drinking its wine, its cider, its milk, its water;
fraternising with its soldiers and their women, their children,
    their dogs and their cats;
eating with them, marching with them, enduring with them;
knowing why, when they laughed, when they prayed, when
    they got drunk, when they sobbed.

Together we learned the brave new world,
knowledge for the picking up behind every blade of grass,
in the whine of every shell,
in the pose of a dead horse,
in the human leg without a body,
in the bodies half trampled into the mud,
in the stench of the living among the stinking dead,
in the lull of sunrise after the hell of night,
in effort beyond effort,
in the untruth of truth,
in the courage of a joke,
in the apathy of living on,
in a week that was a month, a month that was a year, a year
    that was eternity, eternity that was a joke.

Together we went back in mind to the brave old world
of Assyrians and Egyptians, of Hivites and Jebusites,
of Genghis Khan and Alexander and Napoleon . . .
and a million others, lesser ones, but of the same trade;

34

remembering that they and we had one thing in common—
the covering of the lands of the earth with our dead;
remembering that they and we used the same words for it—
honor, glory, sacrifice, motherland, fatherland, patriotism,
   God . . .
the same old words, dusted off again and polished up—
inflated currency of the ruling mind,
given high value each time for the purchase of youth;
words only for old mouths, rattling fiercely among the false
   teeth,
words invented for double-dealing since before the coming of
   Christ . . .
And nothing changed, or changing, except for the progress to
   tanks, to flame throwers, to Hiroshima.

PARIS

1. *Before* War

Between the two uniforms there had passed eleven years—
period of acceptance,
of unthinking trying of wings,
crowded, dramatic, overflowing,
as though by right.
One had sipped the heady nectar of Oxford in two hectic
  years of juvenilia;
had learned the weight of London during three years of daily-
  breading;
had twice sailed the Atlantic, to become ecstatically enmeshed
  in the rhythm of the U.S.A.;
had served intense apprenticeship to the pen in terms of
  countless short stories and five young books.
Throughout, there had been spasmodic returns to St.-Malo,
  to bother Père Jean,
shorter trips to Boulogne and Wimereux,
explorings in Dieppe, Paris Plage, Etaples,

a penetration south as far as Marseilles—first taste of the gay
kingdom of Provence.
Throughout, also, there had always been Paris—
Paris for a weekend,
Paris for a special play,
Paris for the chestnut blossoms,
Paris for Paris—
finding quickening, thank God, in the incredible foulness of
the Gare du Nord,
in the decrepit flyblown taxi with an always explosive and
sophisticated driver,
in the feather beds and the damp sheets and the pillows of
rock,
in the walk up because the ascenseur did not march,
in the touch of cognac at an iron café table, swabbed off with
a dirty napkin
and sparkling philosophy,
in the spade-bearded, ankle-tight-corduroy-trousered denizens
of the Left Bank
incapable of life, love, or any self-expression, without their
fervid hands,
in the noonday spate of midinettes, so young, so hungry, and
so articulate;
quickening among chestnut allées alive with candle blossoms,
at bookstalls along the looping Seine under the needle spire
of Notre Dame,
at glimpses into old courtyards whose defaced coats of arms
spelled at least one pace forward,
at the fantastic names of unimaginable side streets,
at the millions of chimney pots, staying in place only by the
grace of God;
quickening, each time, in the realisation of being there,
and being at home there,
knowing oneself sympathetically a part of it all,
pores open,
receiving, delighting,
weighing too . . .
but, each time, storing up.

2. Wartime

Ypres, Lille, Amiens, Péronne, Armentières . . .
and how many more . . .
once, like Paris, cities, alive, hardworking,
once ennobled with cathedrals, Grand'Places, parks,
good homes humming with simple people, jogging along,
believing,
proud of their handiwork, their tradition, their progress.

I knew them all now, but not as cities.
I knew them as piles of broken masonry spilled down the
    slopes of vast shell craters,
reeking sweetly of death;
no people, no homes, no banks, no cafés, no street cars, no
    lights . . . nothing.
For citizenry, now, a few human rats at bay,
fighting desperately from their holes in the ruins;
nothing left to believe in but the glory of war.

Then, unexpectedly, Paris, on forty-eight hours' leave . . .
still achingly Paris to the last chimney pot,
still Paris—but for how long?
One could not tell then if she soon would not be in the path
    of that same glory.
One walked the crowded streets in momentary safety,
rejoicing,
but tight-stomached, bleeding internally,
in one's attuned inner ear the omnipresent crash of destroying
    shells.
There was no ease in orgy.
Nor was there ease within the great doors of Notre Dame
hoping that its stillness would speak . . .
hoping, but not believing any more.

3. After War: Rue Cassette

Before seeing Paris again, a gap of seven years . . .
full years, in the climactic city of New York,
beginning life once more.
Period, this time, no longer of unthinking acceptance, as by
   right,
but grown now, and trying to know;
engrossed in marriage, work, citizenship—
crowning gifts,
more overwhelming in their triple obligation than gold, frank-
   incense and myrrh.
Period, therefore, of search and research
into the upheaved soil of self,
into history again to try and find a moral,
into the value of words that they might not lie,
into the eternal paradox of one's brother man, equally creator
   and destroyer.

New York itself a flaming opal,
giving out the whole spectrum of man's desires;
frenzy crowding lymph;
beauty hobnobbing with ugliness;
magnificence shrugging at squalor;
grasping, a means only to reach again;
all yesterday forgotten,
today torn down tomorrow,
tomorrow already in the discard.

New York itself a floodlighted Marathon
with eight million starters,
each looking for the moment to plant his spikes in the heel of
    the runner in front,
yet all uniting, briefly, to deluge the winners with ticker tape
    laurels as they keep on coming.

New York itself a cluster of quiet country villages,
from old world and new, whose locals fraternise only with
    each other,
breed half-local children,
the other half belonging to New York.

New York itself a distorting glass,
making each rabbit an elephant,
each itinerant swami the savior of mankind,
each best seller the greatest since Shakespeare,
each new serum the cure of all disease,
each gunman Enemy No. I,
each Mayor a Governor of the State,
each Governor the President of the Country.

New York itself a salad of receptivity and the closed mind,
of sentimentalism and repudiation,
of yesterday's formula and tomorrow's approach,
of fear window-fronted by assurance,
of open arms and clenched fists,
of oldest dressed up as newest,

of failure outclamored by success,
of wagons hitched already to stars still undiscovered.

Seven years of steeping in the electrifying ether,
of squirming in crowded bowels of subways,
of enduring subzero winds tearing strips of flesh from the face,
of panting in heat waves straight from the banked fires of hell,
of living in walkups, five stone flights of them,
where newly-weds dig themselves in for the attack on New
  York—
writers, bombarding the magazines, dreaming the great American novel;
columnists, doing a daily grind, their sights set on the theatre;
artists, publishers, poets . . .
some already with babies,
some with babies in the offing,
some with talent, some with less,
but all young, doing, giving, self-believing, friendly,
sharing messes from cans cooked up in kitchenettes,
sharing also their laughter, their eagerness, their tears and
  their courage.

Treasure for a lifetime in this seven-year striving,
rich in fellowship and understanding,
in pride of being accepted, of belonging,
in the inner always-growing knowledge that one was forever
  home.

And then, for winter's interlude away from home, Paris once
  more;
not, as usual previously, alone, or with a brother,
but now, married, therefore life all changed, resplendent with
  banners;
not, this time, in a Right Bank hotel bedroom,
but across the river in the Rue Cassette, in a student apart-
  ment
looking down upon the chestnut trees behind the gray walls
  of the Carmelite Convent,

seeing, too—all Paris spread out in between—the high white
   sparkle of the Sacré Coeur.

Cowpath in Roman times, perhaps,
the Rue Cassette comes meandering down from the gardens
   of the Luxembourg.
For neighbors all around we had kings and their dwarfs,
queens and their lovers,
massacred priests, anonymous, uncanonised,
the Three Musketeers and their carving knives,
all in any of the moonlit courtyards of a hundred palaces.
For other neighbors we had four Siamese kittens who miaowed
   at us from the balcony across the street;
we had a Freudian wineseller in the Rue de Vaugirard,
whose standing joke, every time we dropped in for another
   bottle of wine,
was: "Et l'amour aujourd'hui? Ça dure toujours?";
we had an Italian cobbler who mumbled Genoese through a
   mouthful of nails
when we showed him what Paris had done to our heels;
we had a thousand authors waiting for us at the bookstalls
   round the Odéon;
we had the founders of new schools of painting at the Dôme
   and the Rotonde;
we had a group of Russians at the Brasserie Montparnasse
whose balalaikas poured the Volga into the Seine;
we had the flower of world youth covering the tables with
   their books in all the cafés of the Boul'Miche.

We saw Fernandel in his beginnings,
Cecile Sorel in her never-endings,
the Guitrys and Yvonne in their romantic chatterings,
Josephine Baker in her nude young twitchings.

We heard the first songs of Lucienne Boyer,
the earliest magic of Rafael's concertina,
the intestinal violins and cymbaloms of a hundred Hungarian
   gypsies.

We read the final profundities of Romain Rolland,
the initial monthly Maigret of Georges Simenon,
the young Jules Romains before he became God,
the not so young Proust in his inescapable sickness.

We absorbed the Louvre and the Salon,
the Grand Guignol and the Comédie Française,
the Opéra and the Salle Pleyel.
We mastered the Métro.
We learned the arrondissements.
We became clients de la maison in many a café.
And we made it all ours again,
street by street,
mile by mile,
day by day,
under the pearl-grey winter skies.

Month of April,
month of the first terrific bursting of all growing things,
month of unrest and irregular pulse,
month of good intentions, and old ideas that look absolutely
    new.

Month, this year, of rain and cold and wind-lashed streets;
of great squirtings of water from the shuddering wheels of
    taxis and elephantine busses;
of great nose-blowings and coughings and sudden sweatings,
    a little temperature running all the time;
of the bottle of aspirin, and another of grog, within reach of
    the shaking hand,
so that creaking legs and aching back might respond to the
    urging up one old remembered street and down another.

How could we spare time for bed after twelve years' absence,

after another war and an "occupation,"
after having had it dinned into one's ears by all the pundits
   that France was "kaput"?

Have they seen, these learned ones, the crowds at the foot of
   the stairway,
hatless, silent,
before the floodlit Winged Victory?
Have they seen the marble plaques, flower decorated,
set in the wall of the Orangerie,
in eternal homage to resistance at the price of death?
Have they seen the thin old women of France,
bent and twisted,
still doing, each, the work of two men?
Have they seen the olive trees being tended,
the vineyards being restored,
the new terraces of orange trees—
work of stretched muscles and profusion of sweat?
Have they seen the shelled towns rising Phoenix-like from
   their ashes?
Have they seen the new paintings,
heard the new music,
read the new books?

We make no claim to punditry.
All we have is our impressions,
gathered among mimosa and oranges and the labyrinth of
   Paris,
living among, eating with, talking to
painters and potters,
writers and musicians,
teachers of languages,
makers of movies,
keepers of shops,
young ones just married,
old ones with grandchildren,
abbés in stone-cold churches,
children returning from stone-cold lycées,
returned men from prison camps.

We had met health of mind and body.
We had met planning and dreaming, ambition and work.
We had met enjoyment and laughter.
We had met life.

5. Gargoyles of Notre Dame

Messieurs les Gargouilles, permit me a question . . .
At ease upon your high parapets these eight hundred years
in the topographical centre of Paris,
therefore centre, also, of the educated world suckled at her
    ever-wet breast,
you have remained transfixed, looking down;
and, in watching your own people,
you have watched us all,
learning, in the watching, the strange dough of which human
    bread is made.

You have made her yours, Paris,
by day, by night,
in winter's sad snow and rain and fog,
in spring's intoxicating light, leaves coming,
in autumn's warning gold, leaves falling,
in summer's precious sun, life-giving.

You know her, always hair-trigger,
intensely enjoying,
intensely revolting;
banners flying, music blaring,
organ pealing in funeral dirge or for the anointing of kings;
drunk with victory,
choked with defeat,
hidden in "occupation";
in all her days of coaches, sedan chairs, busses, bicycles,
    shanks's mare;
in doublet and hose, in ruffles and lace, in bloomers and melon
    hats, in slacks and shorts,
in soutanes and shovel hats,
in nun's coifs, hiding the shaven head,
in low blouses, hiding nothing,
in rags, students begging for bread and for straw to lie upon,
in fancy tweeds, students in international palaces in their own
    Cité Universitaire.

You know her rich and her poor,
her artists and her heros.
You know her static, advancing,
in her rhythm and in her confusion,
in her complexity and in her simplicity,
in her stultification and in her inspiration,
in her pride and in her terror,
in her bestiality and in her moral striving.

These you have witnessed through the centuries;
noting, therefore, the triumphal sempiternal march of twin
    gods,
hate and fear,
commanding our worship, our faces flat upon the ground.
You have seen reason outreasoned,
done to brutal death,
its mangled ghost limping in the byways,
crying to be born again.

You have seen beauty bud in our intestines,
flower as the work of our hands,
only to be mashed in the mud,
made shambles,
by these same hands.

You have seen us turn Christian, with loud lips,
knowing us for pagan in our hearts . . .
else nation would not rise against nation,
nor church against church,
nor any man against his brother.
You have seen us ride the tumbrils obstinately to the gallows
for an idea;
you knowing that the gallows is only another idea,
momentarily more obstinate.
You have seen us tire of fatuous royalty;
seen us, the sovereign people, making fatuous tragic holiday . . .

Messieurs les Gargouilles, my question is therefore simple.
Is it your watching of the human race in travail
that has put the leer upon your faces,
has caused them to twist in such outrageous mirth?

Yet, I pray you, keep on watching.
If you have enjoyed the trees in their annual blooming—we
planted them.
If the fantastic skyline of Paris still pleases you—we built it.
If the sounds of life that come up to you mean anything—we
make them.
If, among the gardened walks, the flowers and the fountains,
our children can move a slow inch forward—we fathered
them.

6. Café de la Paix

Focal point of the over-civilised world.
All that is needed is the price of a coffee,
and a tip.
Add what you, yourself, have brought in your unfillable rag-
    bag of collection and recollection through the years.

Within, plush and gilt and bursting Cupids like overpacked
    sausages.
Add mirrors, wherever wallspace offers,
and chandeliers dripping with a million lights.
Without, chairs and tables, aligned in tight rows,
staring and stared at.
Add dust, remorseless as the flapping napkin.

Simple formula for the superlative.

Take the chairs . . .
Male or female, you crawl over your neighbor, with suitable
    apologies,
you hear your neighbor,
you smell your neighbor,
you suffer your neighbor,
you whisper because of your neighbor,
you bear away the curiously lasting impact of your neighbor's
    minor, but revealing, habits
of looking,
smoking,
drinking,
employing hands,
petting hair,
adjusting brassière,
scratching,
crossing and uncrossing legs,
sniffling,
being.
Only marriage offers more.

Add color:
the immediate primary color of sun and shadow,
of old buildings,
of flowers around kiosks,
of skirts,
of trees,
of hatless hair and gaudy shoes,
of faces, of laughter, of life.
Add also the further secondary color:
of skyscrapers,
of reindeer,
of minarets,
of windmills and tulips,
of Big Ben in the fog,
of the bronze horses on St. Mark's,
of organ cactus,
of gypsy music,

of the Parthenon,
of maté,
of pythons in baskets . . .
blobs of it spattered round the iron tables.

Add also din:
the gyration of the human animal,
without which he cannot function,
enveloped in which he must forever do his thinking,
his eating and his sleeping,
his making of love,
his bringing up of children,
his dying and his getting buried.

Or don't take the chairs . . .
Go inside, on to the tacky plush:
still din,
of eating,
with all the ramifying symphony of clashing dishes, working
    forks, dextrous knives,
of drinking,
with barrage of corks and the enticing glug of first pouring.
Color? Of course:
a different gamme in the electrics,
more suited to the changed psychology of the advancing hour,
with potential lowering of defences,
with frank admission of present and encroaching needs . . .
color,
not so much of bodies, as outside, with their surrounding
    aura,
but, rather, here, color of eyes,
loosing strange complex messages for the deciphering,
emitted unbidden,
tempting to the prospector . . .

eyes, vague, washed out,
needing more than the stinging black coffee,
needing, perhaps, rebirth;

hard eyes, frictioned, conditioned, taking no chances;
eyes, innocent, agog, readying for more sights;
unseeing eyes, elsewhere, in some private stratosphere of good
or ill;
bruised eyes, not believing any more in anything;
friendly eyes, unhurt, protected, therefore bold, a simple credo
for all to read therein;
eyes that stare and avoid and stare again, measuring, weighing,
reducing to common denominator;
eyes that have looked death in the eye, and are not impressed;
eyes that have been down in hell and have not escaped, nor
ever will . . .

Add, finally, one more thing:
if you would have the sum make sense,
add Paris,
whose gift, though all men come, is not for every one.

If you have it, give thanks.

7. *Boulevard Saint-Michel*

The guards are posted all around.
They, too, served their time.
Once, avant garde, old now,
but believing,
degreed and decorated,
satisfied,
they man the high stone watch towers
of University, of Cathedral, of Lycée—
Sorbonne, Notre Dame, Louis le Grand and the rest—
their weapons more lethal than any machine gun,
slaughtering, with pleasant slowness, down the centuries,
by inoculation in the young mind's bloodstream
of the sweet insidious dripping of their old proved patterns.

Main thoroughfare of this concentration camp,
the Boul'Miche,
lined with genial cafés,

with old bookshops of books old and new,
shops of music, old music and young,
of clothes for "le sporting,"
of art from ancient to today's inchoate,
of lighters and tobacco sweepings for the throat's delight,
of saintly statues and medallions for the rare ascetic . . .
mixture of predigested pabulum for prisoners' palates.

A loud voice said: "Give me the children!"

They are here, the children,
given and self-given,
in all the troubled tenderness of downy beards,
of firm young breasts,
of tieless shirts,
of female slacks,
of sandalled naked feet,
of waving hands and tireless tongues.
They are here in all their fertile soil,
compost,
of hope, ambition, unfolding vision;
in all the potential upheaval of the searching restless mind.

Theirs is the world in all its five-foot shelf,
to discover first,
then to explore,
later to digest,
then challenge;
theirs to make or unmake,
even to remake,
or to destroy.

But the guards are posted all around . . .

See them come, these children,
these great ones,
these prisoners holding destiny prisoner in their chubby
    hands;

marching in on eager dedicated feet
from the earth's highways and byways;
white, and not so white,
brown, and brown that merges into black;
from homeland and far land,
from all the tiers of the Tower of Babel,
seeking, all,
to achieve one code,
one way of life,
one bridge to understanding.

See young Confucius,
released from ideography;
young Einstein,
eyes burning, hair still black;
young Winston,
surrounded, caporal on lip,
flowing with flowery phrases;
young Madame Curie,
bob-headed, all adream;
young Borodin,
rapt at the jukebox;
young Matisse,
sucking at a conte crayon;
already, all, so far beyond;
already, all, so nearly ready . . .
Avant garde again, in the revolving cycle.
And, too soon, guard again,
to man the high stone watch towers.

8. Place des Vosges

Silence first,
hanging,
a presence.
Then, arcades under Venetian red and iron balconies.
In the middle
imprisoned trees throwing leaf patterns on safe perambulated
    babies.

Silence, still,
and the gentle melancholy of a threadbare oriental rug,
colors faded,
pattern barely perceptible,
edges ragged . . .
but you can't bring yourself to part with it.

Under the silence,
like unseen sea,

the remote murmur of the republic going about its work.
Place Royale once,
place down at heel, now,
place patined and poignant, still.

Two chairs,
an iron table,
projected on to the sidewalk outside a humble café;
mute invitation to sit awhile,
to sip a drink,
to watch the puppet show
in this derelict onetime centre of an always crazy world . . .
Watch them, gaudy homunculi, twitch on the manipulated
    string:
crowned heads and their kept women and tumbled bedclothes
up there behind the iron balconies;
under the trees,
courtly pavanes in moonlight and linklight,
dancing stately on the people's bellies,
to stringed music
and the eternal seduction of half naked breasts;
under the arcades
thin sharp-eyed boys with torches,
drunken guards with hallebardes,
sedan chairs in the horny hands of sweating serfs
with a pretty face peeping;
at dawn a different revel in the dewy gardens,
not too slippery for flickering blades and titled butchery,
death the price of a pleasantry, a fancied insult, a woman's
    name mispronounced;
and, mightier than monarchs,
cardinals,
the anointed of some God or other,
plotting to strike down the mighty;
in their pleased ears the screams of scared kings
afraid to die,
up there behind the iron balconies.

Then a small chip in the kaleidoscope,
changing color,
tumbles into new place.

The kings have taken their women uptown with the shifting
    fashion.
The sardonic piper has called another tune
and the regal square becomes vibrant
with neighing of horses,
oaths of ostlers,
of peasants in blue blouses,
of lascivious soldiery and their drunken women;
the fragrance of royalty changed to the sharp ammonia of a
    horse market.

Another chip.

Through midnight silence comes faintly the scratching of an
    urgent quill,
birth pains of a giant in verbal labor,
up there behind an iron balcony.
The square is alive again,
this time with ghosts of ghosts:
Hugo
and all the myriad striving creatures of his brain
loosed through the arcades upon an unexpectant world.
And among the hundreds in counter current,
lesser men, but also big,
crowding to the iconoclastic master's shrine—
Dumas,
pregnant with pageantry;
de Musset,
swathed with verse-cloud;
Daudet,
self-pried from the contemplative peace of his Provençal mill;
Dickens,
on blithe holiday from the fogs of London;
the Marquise de Sévigné,
youthfully penning her crown of gay-colored immortelles.

Silence today.
Only the ping of a child's wobbling bicycle bell in the street's
    safe emptiness;
only a vague word from inside the café;
no sound from the shop of undusted bric-à-brac;
the purring of an ankle-rubbing cat;
the remote murmur of the republic going about its work . . .

And the next chip, when it comes sliding?
Who can foretell anything today?

9. Bird Market

Why do you beat strong wings against the bars, selfish ones?
Man is kind.
He takes you gently from the nets,
puts you in six-inch cages in the sun along the merry Quais,
where, as they stroll,
thumbing over the old books,
letting their happy eyes wander from bridge to bridge along
    the great river,
responding once again to the uplift of Notre Dame,
thousands of passersby can pause to admire you,
to covet you,
perhaps to buy you.

Man is kind.

He gives you protection.
Hawks and cats used to kill you as you toiled to get food for

your little ones.
But not now.
He guarantees you food and drink for all the days of your captured life.
He saves the migrators among you from the awful perils of a two-thousand-mile flight through wind and storm.
He provides you with a comfortable home,
where, in some sunny window,
you can watch the clouds go sailing by;
and your owners will give you the boon of their affection,
as well as food:
for man does not live by bread alone;
and he will seek to entertain you,
to entice you,
with lip-chirrupings and cheerful whistlings,
as you sit, silent, on your six-inch cross bar.

If you will only understand
and yield
and give him of your song,
you can be free—
as free as he is—
for he will gladly open the gate of your cage,
windows shut,
and offer you his finger to perch upon;
and his affection will change to pride,
and even to love,
so that he will grieve when you die . . .
and buy another to take your place.

Man is kind.

In return, then, for all his gifts to you,
you should be glad,
knowing that once in your six-inch cage,
you earn for him,
in his,

bread and a little wine and a caporal to hang on his lip
as he, too, toils to get food for his little ones.

Oh selfish,
must you still beat ineffectual hopeless wings against the bars?

SOUTHERN FRANCE

Land, always, of violence by blood, breeding, climate,
of scorching sun and roaring winds,
of snow-covered mountains and palm-fringed sands,
of stark poverty and squandered riches,
of back-breaking work and cossetted idleness,
of all languages, yet clinging to its own Provençal.

Land, once, of kings and fair women and the normal accom-
   panying brutalities,
of treachery and rape and bloody codes of honor,
of troubadours and their double entendre,
of slavery called, as usual, by another name,
of hatred, as usual, hand in hand with love,
of a racial salad tossed with Moorish dressing and Greek con-
   diments.

Land, today, of lonely hill towns and crowded resorts,
of artists and gigolos and retired colonels,
of shepherds playing pipes and ancient women gathering fag-
   gots,

of Cadillacs and donkey carts,
of exaggerated garishness and bewildering beauty.

It was not given to me at the age of nine to realise that Provence had already set its mark upon me,
had, through Aucassin and Nicolette, touched the undirected antenna of my small being,
causing an emotional storm that never altogether subsided,
that brought me, in my remembering twenties, to Beaucaire,
to see, to feel, to try and catch again the first clean childish rapture.
Beaucaire was blistering in the sun,
feet dangling in the river,
skyline of distant hills blurred in haze,
dogs panting in the shade of buildings,
no children running,
the pulse of work at lowest beat,
only the crickets in feverish activity of drilling song.

To us, basking on a café terrace,
a goblet of cool wine in hand,
appeared no damsel who could have stood for Nicolette.
Instead there came a ragged crone,
bent legs propelling the uncounted number of her years,
a crooked stick in one witchlike scaly claw.
Only her eyes enjoyed full life.
These she turned upon me like twin burning glasses,
the other claw held out, palm up,
her toothless mouth mumbling for the charity of "little sous."

At sight of the small pile of silver I put into her hand,
tears made a devious way down the sunken ridges of her cheeks;
and then, with generosity far exceeding mine,
she smiled, gave me words she might have used
if Aucassin himself had tossed her a piece of gold:
"Que Dieu vous bénisse, Monsieur . . . et bonne chance avec la beauté!"

In Avignon, too, there had been such a moment.
We came to it, for the first time, at dawn,
a pink-gold fortress,
as hushed in sleep as all the long-dead popes,
to whose gigantic palace and towering basilica,
already throwing jagged shadows across the square,
we found our way on bewitched exploring feet—
feet which only six hours previously
had trod the raucous ways of Folies Bergère and Gare de
    Lyon.

A yawning waiter staggered from the door of a café,
facing the new day,
broom in hand.
reluctant;
turned upon us tacky barely opened eyes;
produced two chairs on which we might wait for the coffee
    that we could already smell.

The only sounds were leaves in a beginning breeze,
sluggish swish of broom on pavement,
not even, yet, the gurgle of water turned on to run down all
    the gutters.
And then, suddenly, into the faintly stirring silence
came music . . .
a thousand years old,
yet unbelievably private,
as though we had no right to be listening,
to be there;
as though, prisoner behind dungeon walls,
in some cobbled side street of the town,
Pan, through his reeds, were crying for freedom.

Soon, coming nearer, the staccato clatter of unshod hoofs,
muted castanets;
and from the mouth of the street,
flowing like a brown river,
came massed goats,

their young in double time, to keep up.
The music, liquid and formless as a waterfall,
flowed with them,
and from them into one's veins and bloodstream,
so that there was no more any city square,
walled in with ramparts and tombs of popes,
but only solitude in cold nights, dripping stars,
solitude in burning noons among the wild scrub,
solitude, and the long half-thoughts that cannot be spoken,
that change the look in a man's eyes.

The goats, incessant,
serene in their century-old understanding,
left just space enough around the goatherd's striding legs.
He walked, in the close brown stream, as though upon a moving islet;
legs encased in string-tied sacking,
bramble-torn rags hanging from his lean body,
on his head a wide-brimmed conical hat.
Against his body rode a kid,
its head lolling out from the rag folds at his chest.
Long beard and moustache hid the pipes at his lips.
Half man, half Pan, his eyes saw nothing of the city streets.
They were out already beyond the looping Rhone to the far
   hills.

All crossed the square,
entered another ravine of unhearing houses;
and, too soon, time, which had stood still, went on again . . .

The waiter,
slave of cigarette ends, coffee-slopped saucers, insulting tips,
shrugged a shoulder in Pan's direction,
began to sweep again, and said: "Quel sacré métier, hein!"

AVIGNON

Sleep on, ma vieille!
All we ask of you now is to gather at your regal bedside,
undisturbingly, but ourselves not undisturbed,
to marvel, in that, almost,
you are unscarred, unwrinkled . . .
you, who have never known peace, either of mind or of body;
you, who have played always Cleopatra to a thousand An-
    tonies.

The mark must have been set upon your forehead,
for the sound of the subsiding waters of the Deluge was your
    cradle song;
ever since, tearing winds have roared in your ears;
your countryside knew the scourge of a devouring dragon,
till a woman saint came to your rescue;
around you fierce rivers have lashed their coils—
servants for your protection against destroying armies ever at
    your gates.

From your slim youth men have desired you,
taken you,

yielding, or by force;
have built harem walls about you,
so that others might not rob them of their treasure—
walls that were, however, scaled.
And in violence you have been cheated,
betrayed,
sold,
seduced,
raped . . .
you, taking it all proudly in your stride.
You have starved.
You have gorged.
You have leched.
You have repented.
You have returned to your rioting.
When the Black Plague tore into you with its ugly hands,
you purified yourself in unbecoming sackcloth and ashes,
loud prayer upon your unaccustomed lips—
but only to the instant of your cure.
Then, promptly, you turned again to fanfare and feasting.

Your Golden Age brought you great lovers,
mooning and sighing all about,
bequeathing you sweet legacy of sonnets;
troubadours came flocking,
to tune their well-paid lyres in your crowded temples of love;
sinners, in satin and lace,
made continuous procession at your table;
saints, on sad shuffling feet,
set up spots of holiness within you,
seeking your conversion.
But how could their seed flourish upon your rock
when you were in full concern of kings and popes?

They came to you, kings,
flabby,
emasculate,
on their knees as penitent beggars;

and you, in your opulence, watched them flagellate themselves
    through the streets
to earn your slow forgiveness.
They came to you, kings,
male,
demanding,
on stallion chargers,
banners flying,
armies at their heels;
and you, smiling at conquest,
took them right gladly to your bed,
knowing that their priceless jewels would soon be hanging
    upon your bosom.

Popes came to you,
insidious,
equally demanding,
banners flying,
armies of cardinals at their heels,
to use and abuse you;
and you, shameless,
received them with open arms,
pleasurably aware that their gifts would have more of present
    earth than of remote heaven,
more of stimulating vice than of tiresome virtue.

Popes fastened upon you,
refusing to let go their stranglehold,
inoculating you with their cultivated corruption;
some with high altars from which God was torn down,
and Golden Calf installed for adoration;
some with high austerity feeding on blood,
making inquisitional torture a sadistic pleasure;
some with high diplomacy steeped in venality,
so that your honor and integrity became words at which the
    nose was thumbed,
simple commodities reserved for the highest bidder;
some with encouraged lechery, within and without the palace
    walls,

so that you stank like an overripe wound,
exuding pus and running down,
infecting all it touched.

Rich gifts for an ever-apt pupil,
on which you grew opulent
and lush
and bawdy
and more cynical
and over-versed in all the finer points of prostitution
of mind, of body, of spirit,
rejoicing in your infamous fame . . .
achieving, presumably, the laurel wreath of your chosen pro-
    fession,
when, at last,
wrenched free of lesser kings and overzealous popes,
you were haled to his throne by an Emperor.

Today, your day is done;
kings all tamed, heedful of our yea and nay;
popes self-confined in their small plot of alien earth;
and you lie spent,
profession ended,
all passion gone—
save only the river and the wind.
For papal heritage you have five jewels,
matched pearls, resplendent in their antique settings,
more cleanly perfect now than then,
keeping you good company in your quiescence:
Villeneuve, dropped from the broken chain of bridge at your
    feet;
the other four not farther than a reaching hand—
Les Baux on its summit of glaring rock,
Cavaillon, Bompas, Carpentras, behind their living shields of
    cedar.

Today no lugubrious wailings of Black Penitents afflict your
    ears;

instead, the cheerful vins d'honneur of those they call félibres,
clamorous as your emblematic grasshopper;
troubadours in modern clothes,
escapists,
dreamers,
happy singers of your lost youth.

Their songs are justified,
for shepherds still pipe their pagan flocks
past popes' grim empty palace
in the moment that precedes the dawn;
at lightest touch of imagination,
the water wheels of the Guild of Tanners,
rusty,
broken,
but still in their sequence in the shade of great sycamores,
might start to creak and turn again;
that playground of iridescent lizards,
the Escalier de Sainte Anne,
where, once, a fig tree,
earthless,
jutted from the wall,
offers still a halfway halt to heaven . . .
from which, breathless, to look back, and down,
upon the unchanged crazyquilt within your standing walls—
unceasing sun-baked rooftops,
uncountable,
making one,
a flat sea, biscuit-brown,
from which, like mute masts of sunken ships,
jut forth the spires of your papal churches.

LES BAUX

Sun,
a turgid molten river down the street of rock;
sun,
resunned by refraction from the walls of rock;
sun,
striping the street with black African shadows in the swoon-
ing silence;
sun,
making a million motionless fruit trees dance till they merge
into the hard haze of horizon.

Mole men,
living in black burrows in the rock,
making a living by sawing and selling rock in the sun;
mole children,
born and bred in the bowels of the rock in the sun;
mole priest,
saying mass in a chapel in the rock, the overflow on its knees
in the sun.

Inn of rock in the sun,
perched on the rocky lip of the Valley of Hell—
itself bestrewn with upthrusting lumps of volcanic rock,
twisted,
misshapen,
tortured,
infernal,
in the sun.

At last, night comes—
a blue hot darkness,
red in it,
perfumed,
legs of heat bugs still rubbing,
sky ablaze with near stars that tempt a plucking hand,
dogs afoot again,
gathering,
silently suppliant,
edging ever nearer the table on the inn's terrace of rock;
padding of unseen rope-soled feet up the rock street;
voices: jets of Provençal;
the poet-Mayor, félibre,
at our table, unexpected,
declaiming his verse under the hanging stars in the lilting
   tongue of Provence,
repeopling the immediate unbelievable world with legendry
   lovers,
separated,
struggling;
recreating the sad dead children of the gay Queen Jeanne;
recounting Pan and all his tricky fauns out on the rocks.

Then shock of poet's daughter,
most unexpected of all,
coming,
sitting close,
not listening,
reaching out with questioning eyes of troubled black velvet . . .

86

herself most troubling in her urgent Saracen loveliness:
herself, knowing or not knowing,
awaiting, open-lipped,
the snatching of some lucky faun.

Then, all poems done, goodnights,
and silence closing in like the dogs
and emptiness filled with the unrest of her lingering perfume.

How, therefore, could there be sleep for an unlucky faun?
So, a swift climb,
sleepless,
unrestful,
up the sleeping street of rock
to the precarious summit
and the castle's crumbling bat-squeaking emptiness,
alone . . .
in the slow hot aching night . . .
and stupid shooting stars . . .
and, at long last, the release of another sun.

THE CÔTE D'AZUR

Take ten winters up to 1938,
add one more in 1950;
spend them all along both shores of the Mediterranean,
increasing your French,
struggling with Spanish,
venturing even a word or two of Arabic.

Your taste buds will have been stimulated,
for a comparative minute each,
by Rabat and Casablanca,
by Algiers and Alexandria,
by Cairo and Constantinople,
by Jerusalem and Athens,
by Dubrovnik and Fiume;
and the strong fumes of them will curl around your brain,
work their way in,
never leave you.

From Naples to Madrid, however, is another story.
You will have paused here and there,

long enough to pick and choose, to weigh, to make comparison,
to reach decision as to where your soul is best invited.

For you, it might be Taormina—
if you have read your Sappho, and liked it.
It might be Palma,
on its island of melody.
It might be Cannes,
if you like decorum with your seduction.
It might be Monaco,
with its touch of Midas and a littler king,
its yachts and sporting clubs,
its mink and makeup,
its Christian Dior and Pagan Cocteau.

For us, after due apprenticeship in Nice,
it was the mimosa-dripping hinterland of hill towns,
strung like ancient jewels on a knotted string of road,
hairpinned,
up breathless jaggedness and down,
slopes cascaded with olive trees and burning oranges,
hushed,
so that the barking of a far dog,
or the shrill cry of a child,
comes at you from the depths of the soft green valleys
muted and clear.

Up here is the old life,
measured as a pavane,
continuing today the tasks of other centuries,
on the same pieces of earth,
up and down the same cobbles,
in the same battlemented villages,
speaking the same soft Provençal;
roots holding proudly as the millenial olives which once they
  planted.
For music

they have the eternal plash of fountains in their tiny squares,
the clamor of their children,
the flute and the tambourinette,
the nightingales.
For color
they have the play of sun and cloud across sky, mountain and
    valley,
the changing distant sea,
the flowering of trees,
the joseph-coated stucco of their homes.

Ten winters among them, well spent;
receiving kindliness,
making small adventure and discovery,
living always with beauty.

And now, one more winter added,
after "occupation,"
with its grinding hunger,
its frustration,
its revealing inequalities,
its terror,
its subtle humor,
its resistance,
its loneliness and togetherness . . .
gone now,
shrugged off as though remote as Greeks and Saracens;
for, as always, there are mouths to be fed—
and they are feeding them;
work to be done—
and they are doing it;
the dead buried and life to get on with—
and they are indeed living.

Yet always, for us, in that span of years,
Nice was our point of attack, point of departure, point of
    return.
Blindfold we can walk its streets, new town and old;

have seen its changing front;
know its unchanging habits;
have won friendships not alone of French,
but of Dutch and Dane, Italian, Swiss, Hungarian;
have grieved there when death has cut one down,
rejoiced when a new birth has added to their number;
stood god-parents to a girl-child, now in the flush of bilingual
    womanhood;
have recovered there from minor illness,
played golf and tennis in minor tournaments;
spent countless hours there at work, on paper and on canvas;
have made glad holiday each wedding anniversary . . .

O Nice,
we have been like drowned rats in your cold hard rain,
have crunched through your streets in a foot of snow,
have floated along your streets in balmy sun.
We know your churches and your barrooms,
your museums and casinos,
your restaurants and tearooms,
your art shows and your junk shops,
your movies and your busses,
your bookshops and your Galeries Lafayette,
your wineshops and your pharmacies.
We have been passed from desk to desk in your Préfecture,
have waited in interminable line in your post-office,
have signed a million papers in your Bureau de Police,
have subscribed to your newspapers and checked intermina-
    ble inventories in apartments,
have paid the many taxes tagged on to the weekly hotel bill,
have left the little more on the plate after the waiter's per-
    centage has been included on the bill,
have tipped theatre attendants and bus conductors,
sommeliers and concièrges,
head waiters and chasseurs,
croupiers and dames de pissoir . . .
and now make glad acknowledgment that your gay thread is
    inextricably woven into the skein of our lives.

94

NICE

1. *All Things to All Men*

In the beginning was the hill, sheer from the sea.
You built a fort on it—castle, bastions, redoubts,
and were ready for all comers.

You could stop them from the sea;
a broad river guarded your western flank;
the road along the shore from the east was under your battle-
    ments—
scarcely attractive to an invading army;
for ally on the north you had the high Alps with their frozen
    passes.

Nevertheless, all came—
man being what he is, and always will be, world without end,
    amen.
Therefore blood inevitably poured down your slopes,
and death was as the snapping of the fingers,
then, as now.

You beat off fleets,
stopped invaders in their tracks,
tossed stormers from the tops of your walls.
Even your women took a hand at that,
as their later vigorous sisters at other barricades.

You took simple pleasure in it all,
erecting statues to your heros . . .
as we took pleasure in the bombing of Berlin,
as we take pleasure in staring at the girl on the high trapeze
    if there be no net underneath,
as we await the swinging fists and sticks without which no
    hockey game can be enjoyable . . .
for of such is the brotherhood of man.

Yet human desires shift as a weather vane;
and what, after all, doth it profit a man to gain many victories
    and suffer the loss of his own trade?
Your spirit was too fiery,
your defences too strong,
the need for commerce too great.
You were stubbing your own toe,
and the toes also of the founding fathers of civilisation.

On being conquered at last, you found enlightenment,
fell into line,
took down your forts, your walls, your redoubts . . .
and were ready again for all comers.

And again they came, in their hordes;
not, this time, bearing arms,
but wallets bulging with gold.
Thus was your wisdom made manifest.

In such substantial fashion did this golden light of civilisation
    burst upon you,
that soon the huddled outcrop of habitations—
squeezed tight from hill top to river bank,

and housing serf and liegelord, lean cheek by bloated jowl
split at the seams.
The end of the rainbow, where lay the obvious pot of gold,
was across the river.
So, across the river, hurried bloated jowl,
leaving lean cheek,
in his sempiternal need,
to turn discarded palaces into tenements.

Once across the river,
the endless lovely land lying out in the sun
called for your raping;
the restless sea itself was bent to your desires;
the noble stream, grown outmoded as defence,
bridged over, bottled, put to work.

Dawn became the blaze of day.

Great Queens from the land of drizzle
brought their unroyal sniffles
and sat their royal buttocks upon your suburban slopes;
there, condescending to gaze with watery eyes,
upon the ineffable blue of the now healing waters of the Bay
    of Angels.
Then, indeed, were you flushed with victory,
the spoils richer than those which won you your Greek
    naming.

Today,
having swallowed and survived the bitter drench of "occupa-
    tion,"
the outrageous gear of war now rusting on a scrapheap,
you are yourself again . . .
suave,
smiling,
sophisticated,
unperturbed,
ageless as a croupier in your realistic philosophy.

Once more your streets are paved with two-legged gold.
Why, therefore, shouldn't you raise a sceptical eyebrow,
shrug a sloping shoulder,
impervious to the odd discovered foibles of alien visitor,
of native chevalier d'industrie,
both finding their daily way to the police blotter . . .
or not, if you see fit.
Shorn lambs should learn without bleating to gauge the wind's
    temper in the pursuit of pleasure;
for pleasure is your business.

It is for pleasure that they come to you,
all races,
all classes,
all tastes.
And for these do you provide all things,
indoors and out,
grand luxe and no luxe,
discreet and indiscreet,
restrained and raucous,
high-priced and gratis.

Polloi and upper crust can pick and choose,
reject or swallow,
mingle or shun;
the menu endless,
the diet rich:
hushed gambling room and roaring carnival,
dress clothes and shorts,
dancing and horses,
lotteries and women,
acrobats and gigolos,
theatres and bus tours,
caviare and sausages,
low bars and hot nightclubs,
juke-boxes, symphonies, roller-coasters,
diamonds, flea-markets, fur coats,
liquor, sun glasses, postcards,

alpha,
omega.

Today,
your higher slopes, now much farther afield,
are still the prerogative of fast-losing royalty,
whether of crown or kroner.
There, in the lush secrecy of private pools,
do they swim and lie atanning,
safe from the gaining demos on the stony city beach
in frizzling oily masses,
offering happily their curving nearnakedness
to the sun's sweaty all-enveloping embrace.

Across the way from these
in terraced cafés on the Promenade—
flower gardens of striped umbrellas—
lilted with stri.ged music,
are seekers of other pleasures,
male or half male,
with their females,
sipping gay-colored drinks,
soft and hard, like themselves;
more learned, undoubtedly, in their sense of seeking;
preferring the unsweaty female body
clad enticingly in little but the cunning plunging line,
from which soft unprisoned bosom may make planned and
      sweet escape.

Look where it may, indeed,
in all the sun-drenched length of your blue-domed seaside
      Promenade,
the wandering eye,
discerning,
is pleasurably satisfied:
form and color omnipresent,
on beach and in café,
in puffed-clouded sky,
in the stark clean whiteness of your palaces,

in the extravagant palms upthrusting from their beds of
    flowers,
in the soft cool green of the gravelled garden where pink and
    petted babies play,
in the ever-hungry seagulls screaming where the caged river
    bursts its bonds at last,
in the line of painted fishing boats drawn up on their sides
    after the dawn's catch,
in the high green crown of the Castle's hill where lie the dead,
in quiet,
in the lonely shade of a million watching trees.

Yet, if that were all, it would be nothing.
Happily, there is more than the great curve of seafront,
sparkling as brutally as any diamond.
That, after all, is merely your showcase,
designedly unprivate.
What you keep to yourself,
what you are, perhaps,
behind the mask that you wear for the carnival of everyday,
is not there in the open vulgar tray.

It is tucked away,
inland,
behind the hotels,
behind the neon lights,
in quiet streets where royal palm yields to common sycamore,
and Cadillac is dwarfed to Simca,
and mink loses to lapin.
It is in your quarter of homes and neighbors and unfevered
    pulses,
where, daily, the well-scrubbed child, besatcheled, plods his
    way to school;
where women, pausing from the household task,
may kneel,
believing,
in the recreating hush of cold churches;
where youth, big with dream of Sorbonne or Ecole des Mines,

spends lonely evenings in the crowded company of books;
where artists, real or would-be,
arrived or struggling,
facing grimly north,
splash southern color on their canvases;
where paterfamilias, making his own echo in the empty streets,
may safely air his dog before going to bed with his wife.

These you do not advertise—
the unsellable things, having worth and endurance,
deep-rooted in your French mores,
finding expression in oldtime forms and formalities
that exasperate,
that endear,
that tempt the satiric pen of your dramatists:
the wax-polished salon with stiff chairs against the walls;
the Sunday dinner en famille at the restaurant, napkin under
   chin;
the five o'clock goûter, standing up;
the soul-swelling music of the Chasseurs Alpins;
the inviolability of daughters;
the initiation of sons;
the evening promenade, mouth-covered;
the vin d'honneur, with oratory;
the weekly session at the Casino Municipal . . .
how many more that spell such hard words as duty, integrity,
   character?

Lastly, as in the beginning, there is still your Old Town,
where lean cheek was left behind.
He is still there,
swept a little and garnished,
but forever the hewer of wood and the drawer of water in the
   land of others' plenty.
On iron legs, his life is up and down the same precipitous
   rabbit warren;
upon his shoulders the mountains of food that feed the others
   across the river.

With subtle humor, he has not removed the hollow motto
deep carved in stone by his liegelords—
"God is my hope"—
his, perhaps; never theirs.
For him no Chanel Five and Symphony:
only garlic and accordéon;
nor the feminine grace of a Battle of Flowers along the lush
    Promenade:
only the sweaty mob in the neon lights and calliopes along
    the river bank.

Within his strict boundaries,
more social than topographical,
he has learned, perforce, the brotherhood of man—
of Gypsy, Arab, Greek, Italian—
driftwood of the Mediterranean—
even of Chinaman,
whose only expectation of return to homeland
is inside a cheap box of wood.
Brotherhood that squirms, swarms, multiplies;
and should there be ten to a room
within the marble tenement carved with the name of God,
what of it?
Does it not make for company,
warmth,
laughter,
love . . .
and the swift lethal play of the treasured knife?

Where, in the centuries, his women left their washing-boards
to assist in heaving attackers from the walls,
today they stand elbow to perspiring elbow with him in the
    cobbled markets;
experts, all, in the science and art of hard living—
art that knows not the refinement of a north light,
but the constant blaze of a southern sun;
knows not the timid pressure of a studied monotype,
but the violence of all heaving nature,

mirror to their own.
Color is their life:
in explosive slangy patois, untainted by past subjunctives;
in swift interplay between love and knife;
in the stuff itself of their daily labor;
their canvas—
stretched from dawn to noon—
the maze of streets and markets,
covered and uncovered,
through all the winding length and breadth between Port and
    Paillon . . .
gaudy living canvas,
daily splashed on
with unnumbered tons of multicolored vegetables;
touched in with pinks and whites and blues of fish
that slide and slither on their slabs;
bedaubed with yellows, greens, reds, of fruits in vast piles;
blazoned with a billion flowers that burst from baskets,
riot in banked massed tiers on wooden stands,
dwarfing those who buy and sell,
flaunting their magnificence against the old gray walls . . .
Pure color these,
with aching backs and broken hands,
for all the rest of Nice to see, to smell, to enjoy, to afford,
and to bear away in triumphant armsful across the river—
today,
again,
leaving lean cheek and his woman behind.

2. Jewish Cemetery

On the top of Castle Hill
lie the favored dead:
their only disturbance an addition to their number.
Otherwise, silence.
A lizard basking on the warm slabs.
Clouds forming and passing.
The good sun.
Soft rain.
Sun again, drying.

Perpetual candles burn—
the upthrusting green flame of still cypresses.
Flowering shrubs, blooming and falling,
mark off the slow seasons.
Gay bouquets, freshly cut,
daily renewed,

contribute their gaudy moment of memory.

By day,
a guardian walks among them on brotherly feet.
By night,
gates,
unclimbable,
chained and padlocked,
ensure the gift that only their dying brought—
security.

Lucky dead . . .
You need never know
why, for so long,
the welcoming earth has not been upturned among you;
why, in the fullness of expectancy,
wives, daughters, sons, brothers,
will never join you in their allotted spot of holy ground;
why, in the fullness of civilisation,
their tortured bodies have gone up in senseless smoke;
why, instead of digging,
lesser slabs are placed on top of yours,
each carved with the name of your kin
and the place of their shameful slaughtering—
Auschswitz.

Big with conquest,
very correct,
they held a carnival, the grey ones.
From the Place Carnot they came,
marching . . . marching,
arms full swing,
to the measured stamping of the goose step.
And in their midst,
incongruous,
out of rhythm,
hands tied,
two loose-limbed youths, ashuffle,
in the Avenue of Victory.

A halt was called at the Galeries,
busiest place in the town of Nice,
and the grey ones blocked the cross streets off,

held all traffic,
shoppers too,
women and girls in shorts and slacks
in the sun that shone upon them all,
in the Avenue of Victory.

One each side of the crowded street,
they set two poles in the soft asphalt,
each with an arm to hold its man.
And they gave to the neck of both of the boys
a handsome collar of rope,
with a knot for each, below the ear.
And then, with their ankles duly tied . . .
they were always very correct . . .
they hoisted them up to the tops of the poles
as a sign for all to see.
And guards were placed as they dangled there,
two dead boys,
exposed for days
in the sun that shone upon them all,
in the Avenue of Victory.

The grey ones are gone.
Countless poles
without any arm
fly streamers and flags that flap in the breeze;
and massive floats with a king and queen
and a hundred figures to make you laugh,
roll past the crowds that line each side.
And plaster flies
and music blares
and the girls look sweet as they dance along,
free as air in the shining sun,
in the Avenue of Victory.

But on the wall of the Galeries . . .
"Passerby, bow your head!" . . .
and other walls in many a street,

is a marble stone with names and dates
as a sign for all to see.
And each one tells of a boy who died,
with a wreath to show they are not forgot . . .
"passerby, bow your head!" . . .
like the two who hung,
exposed for days in the shining sun,
in the Avenue of Victory.

4. Casino Municipal

You watched Narcissus at the pool,
and learned the reason.
You were among the elders who took a peek at Susanna,
not with licking lips,
but quietly,
with wisely nodding head,
drawing conclusions.
You put the two together and multiplied by millions,
deducting fractions of this and that,
and your answer was correct.

You are, thus, the cerebral and the intestinal.
Your gospel is the recognition of values.
You understand trespassing signs
and their placement,
and the essential purpose of barbed wire.

You know the simple things:
that goodness, if too good, is bad;
that badness, if too bad, is worse than too-goodness;
that the scaled dose of each,
skilfully combined,
is essential in nature.

You are, thus, dedicated to service.
You cater.
You relieve.
You set up.
You are a safety valve.
You are a disguised form of confession on Saturday nights.
You are a family affair.

From decade to decade they come to you,
habit-formed;
and your vast halls change not,
nor need they,
save only for a coat of paint,
a new chair seat,
a new waiter.
Your clientèle changes only in that sons grow up,
marry,
bring accustomed wives,
sweet wide-eyed daughters, growing—
grandpère's delight—
none ever in any jeopardy from hot eyes that go seeking,
from lascivious fingers pinching tender startled behinds.

You did not need even to rule out the mistress,
the pimp,
the street walker,
the gigolo:
since these, you knew, work only in greener pastures.
For your ancient changeless program
is not meat for these stronger-stomached ones
who have climbed out from behind the barbed wire.

For them the fandancer,
the strip tease,
the all-pervading flesh.
For you and yours the immemorial family formula:
discreet indiscretion;
a note;
a touch;
a hint;
a smile, but no belly laugh.
The little less and how much more it is!

Your girls, therefore, are never naked—
a bare leg, perhaps, beyond Toulouse-Lautrec.
Your music is never bebop—
only the skim-milk-six-proof stimulus of a Straus waltz.
Your tangos have been tamed,
diluted,
degauchoed;
your rumbas purged of the abdominal and the posterior.
On these, all, you keep incessant guardian eye,
lest there be moral stone for gentle foot to dash against.
Rather, for you, the unbruising tapping of mother and daughter
to basic rhythm of tempered African.

Hence, your spectacle can be watched unblinkingly,
without a skipped heartbeat,
without disturbing blush,
by father, mother, daughter, son,
over their sirops,
their orangeades glacées,
their café cognac,
even their slug of Scotch.

Since time was not, you have employed a slave gang of jugglers,
strong men,
trained dogs,
acrobats,

lassoers,
trick cyclists,
contortionists,
trapeze artists,
tumblers,
balancers,
ball room dancers,
diseuses,
seals,
knife throwers . . .
gathered from all races,
performing the same acts forever,
given the same roll of drums at the same climactic moment of
    unoriginality . . .
mysterious host serving your need,
trained, God knows where, to expert mediocrity,
to a virtuosity of world-sameness;
performing, throughout that world,
the same humdrum routine to the same humdrum mind—
accepting,
obedient,
satisfied,
unquestioning,
safe in its response to repetition, to cliché;
applauding the known;
silent before the unknown
until it, too, in turn, becomes known.

For full measure, you employ also a minor goddess of chance.
Your nice sense of timing grants to paterfamilias—
whose rond-de-cuir buttock resents at last the unsoftness of
    the unrelenting chair—
a period for the restoration of circulation,
a period of the most attractive,
not only for him, but for you;
period when he may renew himself for further sitting
by standing at your gaming tables.
For him, for you too,

the little ball on the swift slotted wheel,
dances a special rumba of its own.
"Faites vos jeux, Messieurs!",
not an order, but a seduction.
And you do not remind him that the odds are some sixty to
  one in your favor.
You know he prefers seduction to hard fact.
And so, in allotted minutes, you tempt him,
offer him the chance,
the possibility,
the hope,
the potential joy,
of making the price of admission,
the round of drinks,
the pourboires,
the infinite satisfaction of the evening's entertainment free.

And you, calmly dispensing a trifle of loose calculated change,
you can afford a whimsical smile,
for you know that you,
subtle physician,
are the eternal winner,
winner of him and his so long as human character follows its
  norm.

BIOT

1. Road Sign: 4 K.

On the Plaine d'Antibes a million cars,
doing their "cent à l'heure,"
eyes glued,
ears tuned to the humming of rubber,
minds destination-conscious.

Only the million-and-oneth,
knowing,
therefore expectant,
therefore eager,
slows for the small sign: Biot 4 K.,
deserts fast macadam for slow dirt,
to find, at the end of four meandering kilometres, reward,
be it of the spirit, the mind, or the emotions.

A miniature, Biot,
composed,
precise,

volcano-shaped,
pulsing with color,
jutting from a fringe of cypresses and olive trees,
here and there the leaping flame of mimosa,
backed by the blue-green jungle of pines that conceal distant
   Valbonne;
without and within, a painter's dream.

For twenty of its eight hundred years
we had known it,
made it ours this year again,
not, as before, with humbled brush and tube,
but quiet-footed and short of breath into its hushed centre—
untouched by war,
unspoiled by chromium,
unmindful of time.

Roman women still bend over the washing places.
Roman potters are still wet-handed at their wheels.
Grandmothers sit in a crack of sun,
or in the shade of arcades,
their ancient knees pillow-covered,
their gnarled fingers miraculous among intricate bobbins at
   their lace-making.
Old dogs lie stretched on the safe cobbles.
At noon and sundown, on dissonant bells, invisible hands
   announce the Angelus—
signal for a myriad birds to start their evensong . . .

And on the Plaine d'Antibes a million cars whiz by.

2. In the House of God

Little Biot—
rising suddenly steep from the flowery plain
where bold narcissus hides shy cousin violet in the grass,
and the heady orange blossom is tempered by the sea's salt
    tang—
you were among the first to hear the marching feet of Greeks
and, from your ancient tower,
discern the dreaded sails of Moors
and set quick torch to warning smoke-fire.

Kings have passed you by;
but journeying prelates deigned to pause awhile at your gates,
not so much to worship God
as to see if the wine of your vineyards
were, indeed, worthy of their parched holy gullets.

Lately, Huns have held you:
brief insult in your long history.

Today, you slumber in the sun,
remembering,
shrugging an ancient shoulder,
knowing that all things pass.

In your fortress-church are many treasures—
bones of long-dead saints,
dim old masters,
black carved stalls, peopled with impious devils,
and many another dusty relic of the centuries
admired by polyglot whisperers in the crepuscular gloom.

Yet the greatest treasure of them all,
unnamed,
unnoticed,
but undimmed in imagery,
more quick of color than any antique canvas,
hangs at that altar where, at Christmastide,
the Child smiles out from his wooden crib.

It is only a simple unfinished stone of marble,
crudely carved with simplest words.

They tell of an evening in spring,
red sun dropping,
sea a dark jewel,
hills still aflame;
and of a brown-clad monk,
dusty,
tired,
staff in aching hand,
wending down from the woods of Valbonne.

Did you guess then by what happened,
or did you find out later . . .

for indeed it must have been . . .
that those worn sandals bore the good Saint Francis?

Stranger, and alone, he came,
bent to the climb of your steep street,
to be welcomed, followed, by all your cats and dogs in temporary harmony.
Up, past the quiet potters,
still at their wheels while light remained;
up, past the washing women finishing at the troughs;
all pausing from their chatter
to gape and wonder at the strange procession,
some, perhaps, to fall in doubting line.

On up, past the low arches of the cobbled place
went the brown saint and his friends,
to stop at the iron-studded portal of the house of God.
Then, smiling to the cats and dogs, he said:
"Little brothers and sisters,
will you not wait for me awhile here outside?
I would go speak with my heavenly father."

And so, in obedient rows,
all sat themselves upon the cobbles.
But the good saint, having thanked them,
turned, first, towards the woods in the rich afterglow;
and then, raising his voice in summons,
spoke the words now carved and hanging by the Crib:
"Nightingales!
Gentle dwellers in the woods,
before you go to sleep each evening in the thicket,
you who sing so well,
raise up a sweet song
to Jesus your master
who created you!"

Forthwith, from the woods near and far, he was answered.
And in their glorious burst of song
he opened the door of the church—
left it open,
so that God might also share—
and descended the stone steps into the presence of his friend
    and maker.

VENCE

1. Hic Jacet . . .

"Combien je regrette mon bras si dodu . . ."
Only once have we seen you "plump of arm,"
upon a day of festival:
lit up by gay costumes,
shrill with flutes and tambourinettes,
dancing,
marching,
singing . . .
but only that once in all the twenty years that have since
   elapsed.

Must you always go on regretting?
Will you not cast off sadness?
Will you not tell yourself that your present state of suspension
   is only that of a stopped clock,
waiting the knowledgeable finger to set it in motion again?

You cannot plead that life passes you by,
for you are still the inland crossroads,
focal point for grinding busses that crowd your square,
drawing breath for the further climb—
east to Saint-Jeannet, Gattières, Carros;
west to Tourettes and Castellane and on to Grasse;
or ready to slide down the hill to Saint-Paul, La Colle, Cagnes
    and on to Nice.
Hourly, a hundred cameras click at your face—
but you will not smile!
Hourly, a hundred glasses of your good wine descend dry
    throats—
but you will not be gay!
O Vence, what ails you?

2. Prayer to Saints Lambert and Véran

O twin ex-bishops,
saints these many centuries,
godfathers of the town of Vence,
who paraded her streets,
bullied her,
loved her,
died on her bosom;
who, even when dead, deflected the cannon balls of her be-
    siegers back upon themselves,
who gave sight to her blind ones,
who dulled the pains of childbirth for her female citizenry,
who still enjoy carved and dignified repose in the medieval
    gloom of her small but delightful cathedral,
awake, I pray you from your overdose of slumbering!
Make ready all the miracles left in your lockers!
Unloose the strings of your celestial harps!
Leave them upon a dry cloud in the safe keeping of guardian
    angels!

Gird up your skirts and roll your sleeves,
for your beloved town is sore afflicted and cries to you from
   the depths!

Have your eyes been dazzled by unearthly glory?
For too long you have not looked down upon the town that
   gave you earthly glory,
clothed you in rich robes and jewelled croziers,
housed you in palatial pomp,
gave you to eat of its best food,
to drink of its mellowest wines;
gave you, both, moreover,
your chance in life to win to sainthood.

Is gratitude an empty word?
Can forgetfulness be any part of saintliness?
It cannot be that some good Vençois,
passed by Peter at the pearly gates,
has not urgently enquired his way to your stalls in the
   heavenly choir,
seeking to interrupt your harping,
seeking to tell you of your city's straits.
Perhaps, too humble, he was afraid to pluck your sleeve . . .
Lend to me, then, each an ear, O Lambert, O Véran!

I am no Vençois . . .
mere pilgrim from a far barbarian land,
but coming on loving reverent feet these many times;
coming an always ecstatic way from the shore of the sea
to your high site beneath the great "baou";
always up,
winding,
enflamed by oranges, mimosa, almond, all cupping the sun;
with the smell of snow on the eternal Alps;
always up, and pausing at a coil of road,
to look down in happy wonder at your sister town, Saint-Paul,
snugly dormant upon her green rock;
today as true to herself as when you, both,

honored guests,
gave her your episcopal blessing;
always up, to pause again and turn a feasting eye
across the soft green valley that divides your Vence
from the distant craggy fastness that is Saint-Jeannet.

Yourselves, on sandalled feet and countless times,
have trod those very ways,
making the same pauses.
Do not your eyes soften a little at the recalling?
Have you found anything more beautiful
up there in your cloudly kingdom?

I pray you, lean well over for a further look,
not upon this fair countryside—the work of God—
but upon the once fair town of Vence, and see the work of
   man.

There is today no enemy with simple cannon ball and cum-
   bersome battering ram,
with whom yourselves once dealt right handily.
Today your miracles must be directed against a subtler foe,
working from within,
like a pale fat maggot devouring the red apple of faith,
of integrity,
of age-old standards.

Look well, O saints!
See, first, how she is left tired,
dishevelled,
sunk in melancholia.
See how sadness oozes from her stones,
drips from her walls,
is written upon the faces of her inhabitants.
There is no sound of cheerful talk, no laughter.
Walk where you will, only solemn eyes meet yours,
no twinkle in their depths,
no readiness to light at a merry crack,
no willingness to cap it with a better.

Are they not as grey penitents,
moving slowly in a grey town,
impregnating the soul with their grey distress,
painting gloom upon the flowers,
making shadow prevail over sun?

O saints, where is the Vence you knew,
proud-breasted, defiant?
See where, now, in blindness, they have shorn off her outer
    garments,
leaving her with one shameful rag of rampart.
See what they have done to the old enchantment of the Place
    de Peyra,
used now and abused by greedy merchants,
lacking all taste,
plastering their walls with garish horrors,
spewing out their goods upon the polished cobbles beneath
    the giant elm.
See how in the main square the insidious poster,
brazen in appeal,
always lying,
has ousted the vine from the walls;
how the tranquil walks beneath the sycamores
have degenerated into a littered parade of cheapest souvenirs;
how the old delightful curve of the main street
is being debased with chromium and cellophane.

If this were all, it would still be more than enough.
But it is nothing.

Turn now to the Place of the Cathedral,
your Place, O saints,
once made holy by your prayers and good works,
made colorful by your vestmented processions,
made musical by the rhythm of your chantings,
made sweet-smelling by the fragrance of your incense.
Can you recognise it now?

See the mushroomed atrocity upon the foundations of your
    torn-down cloistered bishopric,

its horrific bulk,
broken out with emblems in stucco,
dwarfing your patined place of worship.
Insult? Indeed yes; but not the final one.
Look beyond, to where your once pleasing vaulted passageway
has now been usefully transformed to civic purposes.
Can you see?
Can you smell?
Can you guess?
Shades of you two, whose once honored tombs are there!
Shades of your pious successors: of little Godeau, of Pope
    Paul, even of the hated Leblanc!
What lassitude of mind was here, that it was not—marked by
    kindly arrows—
erected in some discreet corner of the public square,
where hard-pressed tourists pile from a hundred busses;
or in the marketplace, where all and sundry spend long work-
    ing hours;
or in some lower dedicated chamber of the monstrous Town
    Hall—
in which, God knows, its use would constitute the perfect
    expression of opinion?
Not, alas, in any of these was it built,
but in most distressing adjacence to the doors of your cathe-
    dral,
competing with the odor of sanctity,
intruding upon mind and glands . . .

O good saints, how can you return to the tuning of harps?
If you would save her, the time is now!
Give back laughter to her people,
for without it there can be no vision!
Give them back empty bellies,
for without them they can feel no urge!
Give them back pride,
for without it there can be no standards!
Give them back memory,
for without it they will have nothing but the poverty of today!

3. Matisse Chapel

Maestro,
whose restless palette has always kept you searching,
groping,
enraged,
in colored darkness,
there must be a smile behind your eyes today;
for at last,
after ten more years than the biblical span,
you have tapped light at its source
and color, its child . . .
You have harnessed God to your work.

In all your long life you have not cared
if your crude iconoclastic canvases
caused curses or heaped you with reward.
For you, they were mere momentarily satisfying dissatisfac-
tions,

rejections from the knotted intestines of your driven soul,
bloody footprints on your long way of the cross.

To you what did it matter if your women were pin-headed,
chinless,
faceless;
your nudes abortions,
their distorted limbs a parody?
All you wanted was a shape,
however shapeless,
as target for your tubes of man-made color—
these your joy and your despair,
your limitation and your glory,
dog's vomit to which you must ever return,
seeking therein the obstinate reluctant light
that passeth understanding.
For that, Maestro, was the task to which God harnessed you.

And can you tell today if your travail is ended,
when the walls of jasper and of gold,
now rising,
shall be standing erect;
and the blazing sun on the turning earth
shall give motion,
life itself,
to your dreaming?

Soon you will know . . .
And may you then go in peace!

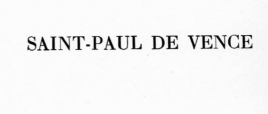

SAINT-PAUL DE VENCE

1. First Time and Always

We were lucky that our car was beetle-sized,
therefore not possessed of a speed demon.
Moreover, uphill, at a purring five miles an hour,
one can cultivate one's garden,
especially such a garden as the road direct from Cagnes to
    Vence;
especially, again, when, for the first time, one is navigating
    towards Eden.

But we were ignorant,
all unsuspecting,
still trailing lower things: impatience, even,
as, snail-paced, we crawled the leafy tunnelled climbing bends.

Only later, as always, did we grasp fully the subtlety of with-
    holding,
the spiritual whetting given by suspense.

High at last upon a ridge, the slow approach was suddenly
    behind,
as suddenly, and forever, forgotten;
for, out there,
below,
above,
everywhere,
lay Eden flowing round Saint-Paul;
beyond all imagining;
sun, sea, earth, running together,
blending,
shaped,
as though God's fingers were still moist with the satisfying
    clay.
How many times, since that first rarest moment,
have we dreamed of "three tabernacles" and their potential
    building!
How many hours, in the course of the years,
have we devoted to the passionate making of daubs of it!
How many days and nights, through a winter and spring,
have we soaked its ambiance into our older bones!
How many friends, inside its hospitable walls,
may safely look for our returning!

2. Town of Many Faces

Local poets, without undue straining,
have likened you to a boat of stone,
patined by the centuries to a battleship grey,
presumably awaiting a volcanic launching
down brief emerald slips
into the expectant Mediterranean.

It could be said that your first class decks
have known the feet of minor kings,
of at least one rampant queen who sold you to the highest
    bidder,
and a ruck,
however resplendent,
of satellite Counts, Nobles and Bishops.
Moreover,
to paraphrase slightly,
the steerage ye had always with ye.

Yet you are much more than boat.
You are mystery and paradox.
You are death and resurrection.
You are survival,
sprawling like a couchant dinosaur,
alive still and vastly healthy,
the number of whose years is far from being told.

Boat of stone?
That is the little less.

Consider.
From below,
you are a mighty fortress,
under whose precipitous walls, the stoutest-hearted attacker,
Phoenician, Moor, or Roman,
must have had the bitter smell of death in his nostrils.

From above,
a cunning child could have built you with a box of toy blocks.

From one end,
you dominate a background of swelling valley,
in whose folds small farms are dots.

From the other,
you are nothing but the excrescence of baby-rock,
plastered against the skirts of your mother-mountain,
salmon-pink where the snow lies piled on the bitter crags.

From one angle,
it would seem that there is neither valley nor mountain,
and you are foreshortened to matchbox-size
against the vast blue of the sea's horizon.

From another,
you are a naked outline,
flat as board,
hard and jagged against the sailing clouds.

When the sun glares on you
you are biscuit-brown,
besplashed with greens, whites and flaming yellows.

When the rain drenches you,
grey is your overall garment.

And when the mists rise,
cloying, encircling,
they invest you in a cloak of invisibility.

Such are some of your many faces.

By simple happenstance
wars have left you unscarred,
externally at least.
Even your recent "occupiers" succumbed to your witchery,
withdrawing, at the approach of the liberator,
without inflicting harm upon you.
And today, under the august wing of the Beaux Arts,
not a stone of your moss-sprouting ramparts may be turned.

Countless tubes of paint have been squeezed
and spread out with brush and knife,
so that you—or what passes for you—
may be found hanging in the world's galleries of art;
while, by those of leaner pocketbook,
your pictures on postcards,
vilely colored or not,
have been sent out to the globe's most unknown corners.

Your legends,
of rutting lords and naughty ladies,
of fighting and feasting,
of pageant and plague,
have been sung and read,
recited and speechified,
with appropriate gesture,

with tears,
and, be it confessed,
during the vinous moments of your spring festival,
with burping and hiccough.

You are converged upon, winter and summer,
by painters, poets, novelists, columnists,
as bees to a comb of honey,
and, like them, go to instant work.
From every department of France they come,
blocking the Route Nationale,
in their eagerness to exchange the dust of their city for your
    magic dust.
From every prison camp in Germany
your children, dying by inches,
have poured out their longing for you
with stubs of pencil on backs of envelopes,
have dragged infinite miles on bleeding feet to see you once
    again.
Today and every day your yard-wide streets
resound to the major and minor tongues of your fanatical dis-
    coverers—
Danish, Spanish, Greek, cockney;
Roumanian, Wild West, Australian, Hieland Scots;
Berber, County Clare, the Deep South, Hindustani.

What, then, have you?
What "better mousetrap"?
What is it that you give that pleases every race?
Your appeal is immediate,
oddly violent,
to eye, to ear, to imagination—
even to stomach.
Yet, although your inns keep groaning boards,
it is of common knowledge that the human stomach,
all over France,
can be well soothed;
and to how few is granted the seeing eye that pierces through

to the other side,
looking and overlooking,
filling in and rubbing out,
forming whole beyond whole . . .
and without which there can be only outline.
Moreover, outline or otherwise,
your length and breadth from end to end can be explored,
even on high heels,
in the brief span of twenty minutes;
despite which, all men beat a pathway to your gates.

Grant, then, that to seeing and unseeing
you are beautiful in yourself, in your setting,
in the successful cooperation between God and Man.
But so also are your sister towns—
Mougins, Gourdon, Saint-Jeannet, Carros, Eze, a hundred
    more.
They, too, perch above basking valleys,
share the same sun,
see the same sea,
are sheltered from north wind by the same snow mountains,
are splashed with the same mimosas, oranges and flowers.
Yet, of them all, only you are Venus.

Like them, you burn in summer; yet only you are mobbed.
Like them, your winter streets, ice-cold, are full of sniffles,
your stone houses torturing the human body
with gravelike chills,
rheumatic stabs,
sciatic daggers;
yet only to you does the tide of pilgrims flow,
befurred,
bescarved,
bewitched.
They park their cars in chromium rows
to see white pigeons flash and whirl in the cold sunshine,
clinging to grey ramparts a moment like giant flakes of snow;
to watch young boule players, intent,

swing graceful arms on the red sand
beneath the leafless sycamores;
to follow a flock of huddled sheep
baaing through the tunnelled gateway
guarded by rusty cannon and the Infant Jesus;
up past the antique shops,
and the barber's,
and the enticing hole in the wall
where, on principle, can be purchased anything from pins to
palm trees;
on up past the singing fountain,
and the cobbler's
and the woodworker's,
and the sculptor of santons,
and the art shops, whose windows are plastered with your likeness and unlikeness,
your distortion and your abstraction;
past stone-escutcheoned doors,
iron-studded,
prideful,
touched faintly with the stale odor of bygone Nobles,
and behind which now, as then,
the same human animal struts his little moment—
happiness and hatred in the same four-poster,
health and misery,
content and jealousy,
poverty and pride,
worker and idler,
communist and chauvinist;
up past all these normal crowded living
and out through the southern gateway
to where the crowded dead,
huddled like the living and the sheep,
are pressed down by gigantic blocks of advertising marble,
upheaved a little, here and there, by kindly roots of cypress
trees
seeking to ease the final pressure.

Since for the quick, too, it is the end of the road,
they then turn back along the western ramparts
to where the mastodonic busses honk and roar,
back and fill to make the hairpin turn
that separates competing inns
wherein the now hungry pilgrim,
may empty fat pocket-book and fill fat stomach.

Brief anabasis:
enchantment and disenchantment at every turn,
yet enchantment never the loser.
Consider your cobbles,
patined but haphazard,
and slippery as glass,
inviting the sprained ankle;
add the steepness of your twisted alleys
and their threat to bursting lungs, to unaccustomed legs . . .
yet bright-eyed toothless crones,
more bent than the canes on which they lean,
navigate freely with the startling speed of crabs.
Consider your garbage,
openly exposed to all the world,
removed in a handcart the size of a wheelbarrow . . .
yet it is pulled by the most delectable of donkeys,
encouraged in his task by an iron-legged grandfather
in the soft tongue of Provence.
Consider your flickering electric lights,
of one generous candle-power,
serving only to keep you in medieval gloom . . .
yet making you, for that, the more romantic.
Consider your water,
piped in from the surrounding mountains,
harder than the rock from which it springs . . .
yet, though it leave the chin unbarbered,
it makes the blossoms of your almonds, oranges, mimosas,
paint bright the green surrounding slopes.
Consider the sum total of your offered entertainment,
an antique film one night per week

in a pneumonic schoolroom,
on chairs of wood that squeak,
causing paralysis to aching unrewarded buttocks . . .
yet outside,
the full moon on your ghostly battlements
holds more of intoxication than all of Hollywood.

Thus far, mere scratching of the surface,
delineation only of what meets pre-prandial eye.
To find an approximation to your answer
one must go deeper,
must linger on your perfumed terraces,
lean elbow on a yard-thick wall,
talk . . . and listen,
letting the hush of you sink in.
Then is it seen,
felt rather,
that within your walls the tree of life
is hung with spiritual contentment,
harmony between man and earth,
between man and himself.
Then is it found
that, while you can tell your centuries like the beads of a
    rosary,
your youth continually renews itself,
in urgency of mind and hand,
in need and ability to create.

Your offspring,
scratching the earth beneath your ramparts,
receive at birth green fingers,
receive the gift of recognising beauty:
therefore is your landscape a constant cultivated masterpiece.
Your growers of flowers—
as if that in itself were not contribution enough—
work also with palette and brush,
giving their flowers permanence.
Your sweaty men,

at evening's return from the terraces,
deliver themselves of ballads
whose music has risen from the clods of fertile earth.
Your tireless women,
whose apparent lot it is to toil at the washing troughs
and wield the subsequent iron,
turn from their finished labor
to give with tube and knife,
untaught,
form and color to their deep imaginings.
Their grown sons,
some, at work day's end,
lay hands upon the shapeless rock,
soon made shapeful with hammer and chisel;
others, by the same dim light of lamps,
taking the great roots of olives,
turn the polished rich-grained wood to vessels of loveliness.

Thus are you, somewhat,
however inadequately rendered,
your mystery unsolved,
endless questions still posing themselves.
Take, for instance, your integrity.
Is it your almost monastic seclusion that keeps it intact?
So few miles away is the roaring world—
to say nothing of the flesh and the very devil—
and the weary flesh,
hot-breathed,
seeking vain relief from self,
comes pouring up to your terraces
in the scented scorching summer nights,
to revel,
to dance,
to drink its brief pathetic fill,
destroying your harmony with its cacophony;
and yet, by some miracle,
the dews of dawn wash you clean again,
leave you yourself,

unsullied,
unimpaired,
withdrawn,
murmurous in your next day's rhythm,
bathed again in simple peace.

Take, also, your ambiance of happiness.
Could it be that which makes your people know, and add to,
  beauty,
makes your pigeons seem puffier and whiter,
makes your sky more deeply blue,
makes your cream-robed priests and nuns pray better in the
  suspended silence of your mountain chapels?
Perhaps it is beyond the answering.

3. A Patron Saint

Poor Clare!
You came all the way from Assisi,
leaving a trail of convents with nuns bearing your name . . .
yet no one cares.
You might well have been a playmate of that Francis
who preached to the birds,
made wolves keep their promise . . .
yet no one cares.
You were recognised once,
canonised,
chosen, among other candidates,
patron saint of this small heaven on earth's loveliest spot . . .
yet no one cares.

Poor Clare!
Why have you no place of honor within the town,
save only a bay of broken wall?

Why are there altars named for others in the church,
but none for you?
What odd thinking was it that made your chapel matchbox-
size?
Was it for lack of room that you were relegated to the public
highway?
Was it to serve civic utility that it was poked in beside an ancient olive mill?
Is it fitting that laboring busses should roar to a stop at your
door,
their evil gases nauseate you,
the eddy and sway of their petty merchantry jostle your ears?
Are you become a mere watcher over letters
that a post-office should be held a suitable neighbor?
What have you forfeited that no one can get in to have word
with you,
since the fourth wall of your cage,
an iron grille,
is always locked?

Poor Clare!
Neglected,
cold-shouldered,
left to the noise, the dust, the blowing leaves . . .
even the cross, surmounting the bell at your portal,
atilt.
Children play noisily at the road corner,
with never a thought of you.
Old men sun themselves silently on the marble benches that
flank your grille,
with their backs to you.
No woman kneels, for however telling a moment, at your
threshold.
No peasant removes his hat to you,
nor crosses himself in passing.
The slow shepherd marches past with his flock, unseeing.
Young priests,

cream-robed, black-shod,
a béret on their tonsured polls,
do not salute you even with a glance.
From above you on the hill,
the good nuns,
your sisters,
busy, chattering,
full of the cares of this world,
cluttered with orphans and their handcart,
turn never a coif in your direction.
Only the full-fed tourists,
not knowing who you are,
take cognisance,
snap impertinent cameras in your face.

Poor Clare!
All the world is familiar with dauntless George,
mounted on a grandiose charger,
lancepoint at dragon's throat.
And baffled old Christopher,
weighted down beneath the colossal burden of a minuscule
    Child,
rides daily in a million luxurious automobiles.
And gay Catherine,
friend of all frustrated females,
has her day of dancing in the streets of Paris.
These, and many another favored one,
find purchasers on medallions,
of gold,
of silver,
of rich enamel;
are carried, with faith and hope,
in pocket-books,
on key rings,
on slender chains lying snug against warm bosoms.
But you . . .
Are you of their number?

Not so!
You do not even rate your likeness on a postcard
for minor stamp-saving greetings hither and yon,
soon to find its completed way into the useful wastebasket.

But since all saints have days,
what of yours?
Are you left up there on your road corner forgotten and alone?
Indeed no.
You have your day,
but day of paradox,
of oddest thinking,
of unintentioned insult to your womanhood.
For on that day,
with gayest carillon of all the heartless bells,
named for you,
'tis George they celebrate—
the male patron—
and, spilling out from all the gateways,
hold male celebration
of wine,
of dance,
of love . . .
before your virgin eyes . . .
Poor Clare!

4. Your Women

You women of Saint Paul, you have nothing.
The others everything.

Consider first these others,
the ones whom you see every day,
those who come as to a peepshow,
in shiny postwar cars,
in nylon stockings,
in undies so diaphanous that they must go to dry cleaner, not
   to laundress,
in dresses by the Duchess's own couturier,
in stilt-heeled shoes with soles of paper,
in mink and beaver,
in lamb and leopard,
in nutria and fox . . .
slaughter of innocents,
tender or ferocious,

to drape a female body,
equally tender,
perhaps equally ferocious.
As to hair,
depending on the toll of years,
the wrinkles that will not be denied,
the taut or sagging muscles,
they choose, in their color-blindness,
the colored way of emphasis . . .
purpling,
reddening,
whitening,
blackening . . .
themselves the peepshow.

From near cities and far
they come by plane de luxe,
by train de luxe,
by liner de luxe,
by cars so de luxe that it were honor and financial privilege
to be run over by one of them.
They have been everywhere,
seen everything,
talk incessantly in many languages—a fluent petit nègre—
have read all the books,
heard all the musicians,
trailed through the world's picture galleries . . .
their culture so complete
that instantly
they can tell a Braque from a Bonnard,
a rumba from a tango,
a Châteauneuf du Pape from a sparkling Vouvray,
a pizza from a peacock's tongue in aspic.

They have husbands,
in tow,
with titles,
without titles,

156

with money,
with more money,
whether they be old or bald,
goodtempered or bad,
drunken or sober,
lean or pot-bellied.
They have dogs,
with pedigree,
without pedigree,
old or bald,
goodtempered or bad,
lean or pot-bellied.
They have chauffeurs,
today's eunuchs,
safe, as driver and as man,
impersonal as carburetors,
purely functional,
impervious to nyloned knee,
to peep of flesh and pants,
when helping Miss or Madam from the car,
speaking only four words in any language:
"Yes, Madam . . . No, Madam."

They have houses,
in town on the best streets,
in the country in the earth's beauty spots;
houses in which science is their footstool, big industry their
    slave.
At the first twitch of a desire,
these twin obedient servants rush to serve,
to satisfy,
to surfeit;
bringing them miracles in bottles and in cartons,
in crates and in cellophane;
miracles,
causing their drying skin to become as the lily;
granting them to breathe freely, without that pictured look of
    horror;

giving them secure gums again, dentures that will not click;
allowing them to sweat without odor;
miracles,
of enjoying food that cooks itself at the turning of a switch;
of enjoying ice that makes itself for their drinking;
of enjoying garbage that grinds itself into disappearance;
of enjoying dust that sucks itself into writhing tubes;
of enjoying laundry that washes itself whiter than fresh-fallen
    snow;
of enjoying air-machines that make winter summer, and sum-
    mer spring;
of enjoying seeing-machines that pluck the insignificant do-
    ings of mankind out of the ether, and drop them, moving,
    into their silken laps.

Thus, therefore, they have everything.

But what, then, have you, women of Saint Paul?
Your day begins with the light and ends with the darkness.
You tread incessantly the hard steep cobbles,
to fetch your water, rain or shine, on legs of steel, from the
    public fountain;
to fetch your food, rain or shine, from the bottom of the hill.
With your two rough hands you cook the little that you have
    to eat.
On your two rough knees you scrub your stone houses.
On a floor of stone you scrub your children in a tub of zinc.
With your two frozen hands you scrub your laundry on stone
    slabs in icy mountain water.
You have seen no art . . .
other than the sunset, the moonrise, the landscape, the pic-
    tures in your shops.
You have heard no music . . .
other than the singing of your fountains, the cooing of the
    doves, the puling of your first-born.
You have read nothing . . .
other than the faces and feelings of those about you.

You have been nowhere . . .
cloistered for a thousand years behind your ramparts,
working,
living;
but your eyes sing
and your smile is an accompaniment,
for that your men are strong in the fields and on the terraces
and that your noisy children will give another thousand years
    to life.

Could it be that you have everything; the others nothing?

5. Cats

Big and little,
tabby and black,
striped and spotted,
well found and rangy,
you all gave added life, color, grace, delight to the eye,
on countless doorsteps in the narrow crooked streets of your
    empire.

My hand went out to you with measured slowness,
friendly smelling,
eager to stroke your chin,
to invite your purr,
to see your eyes close in acknowledging bliss.
I talked to you,
not raising my voice,
in French, in English,
in humble imitation of your own universal tongue.

But you, cats of Saint-Paul,
you would have none of me.

True, I was a stranger in your yard-wide alleys,
but stepping softly
and attuning my behavior to your ways as I had observed them
in cold countries and hot,
in many far lands;
rewarded always with welcome,
and, at once, trust,
and progressing, even, to affection.

But you, Saint-Paulois, on low bellies,
furtive,
shifty-eyed,
tail dragging,
you slunk by in the gutter,
as though my hand held only contamination,
or could dispense only wrath.
You dived into tiled drains,
where, you knew, neither hand nor dog could follow.
You flashed down other alleys,
pausing only to look back
when you had put safe distance between you and me.
You disappeared through broken windows,
up and over rough stone walls,
down into the safe blackness of murky cellars.

What had I done,
or left undone?
Why did you leave me baffled,
a trifle humiliated;
as though, perhaps, I had lost some quality
and was unaware of it?
Suppose, on my return home,
my own cats should shy away from me?

You looked well fed enough, most of you.
Somewhere, in safety,
you had taken time out to lick your coats shiny,
to wash, eyes closed, behind the ears;
and yet, watching you,
it seemed to me that you must have mapped out every inch of
   every alley
against the dreaded moment
when the saving leap would be your dire need.

I saw dogs bark at you,
from accustomed respectful distance,
leaving you not too perturbed.
As you well knew,
a meaning spit, a sweeping claw,
would send most of them yelping.
These, then, were not in cause.
Nor did approaching women divert you from your purposes,
more than to take a swift step from their path.
But when, on hard uncaring feet,
clumping,
making cobbles ring,
men came . . .
then was evident your deep distress,
then was your cathood debased.

A queer thing, disconcerting,
beyond my poor reasoning;
for one had only to note your dignified unhurried possession
   of the family doorstep,
careless of clatter of domesticity within,
to know that you were citzens of good standing,
had earned your place at the fire,
your daily ration,
a lap in which to curl and safely dream of hunting, tail
   atwitch,
had played with rough children,
making you expose protesting claw,

only to make up again
with velvet treading feet and recontented purr.

Many of you I was privileged, later, to meet
inside your houses—
tigers,
blue Persians,
Siamese—
and there, off the streets,
you gave me the full measure of your confidence,
rewarding me with all the charm and lithe graciousness of your
    kind.
But it was many weeks before even you,
now friends,
could differentiate, when outside,
between me, as man,
and me as the man whom you had now admitted to the circle
    of your affection.

What dark business of man had sown the streets with dread,
changing you, in your peaceful peradventurings,
from serene majesty
to slinking subservience?

There came a day when I was called down to the great city of
    Nice,
gleaming white,
hub of all coastal affairs,
honking,
clanging,
traffic-jammed,
bristling with white-gauntleted police . . .
as far removed, apparently, from Saint-Paul
in thought, habit, deed,
as two continents with ocean in between.

But it was there,
in all the riot and confusion.

that I stumbled,
all unprepared,
on the answer to cat-behavior in Saint-Paul.
It stared at me from the display window of a pharmacie,
stomach-turning,
sour-tasting,
remindful of Judas and his counted pieces of dirty silver.

There, tastefully arranged,
so that variety of markings would catch and please the eye,
were laid out skins,
black and white,
blue-grey,
tabby,
tortoise-shell . . .
skins of friends,
who might have curled up on one's knee,
who might have trustingly paraded their kittens, one by one.

A sign told it all:

CAT SKINS

God's gift to the Chilly
    for
    Bronchitis
    Enteritis
    Lumbago
    Sciatica
    Rheumatism
    Shivering Spells

USE CAT SKINS

And the price of betrayal?
A real bargain, for a nice skin, at fifteen hundred francs.
What clearer?

With hard work
and a good eye
and rubber soles
and a deep sack
and a darkish night
and a little luck . . .
a comfortable living for a good sportsman
in the streets, say, of Saint-Paul!

6. The Inn of the Golden Dove

Your name itself is born of fantasy,
a poetic yearning that happily came true;
for your doves are, indeed, of gold.
You are a Provençal Pied Piper,
your notes carrying over mountain tops,
not being stopped at frontiers,
enduring beyond vast oceans.
Greeks hear them,
and Britishers,
Danes, Americans, Italians, Roumanians,
all,
even the rare uncurtained Slav.

Strange music in those different ears,
not understandable, only felt;
harmony and cacophony, twin sisters, intertwining—
music of the fluttering of white doves,

the barking of old tolerated dogs,
dragging of heavy tables,
crashing of thick plates,
clicking of iron boule balls on the red crushed sand,
of utter murmurous quiet,
punctuated,
torn and rent,
by moments of domestic uproar;
grace-notes of multitude and solitude on gentled Alps sloping
    to the sea,
flowing round fortress towers reaching to the sky;
of dark cypresses, and trees all hung with oranges,
and golden branches heavy with mimosa,
of roses by the armful, and giant carnations,
multi-colored,
all splashed by the sun;
of smell and sight of broiling chickens,
gravely turning on an ancient spit;
of the popping of infinitude of corks,
red, white, rosé;
of the rattle of a hundred tongues in as many idioms,
and pausing not in their complacent rattling
when an unhurrying unseeing shepherd
passes at the head of his slow flock,
inserting a note of eternity.

Yet, equally eternal,
if dissonant,
are mink coats towed by tonsured poodles,
young heads of bottled Titian,
old heads of purpled white,
reeking of Chanel's arbitrary Five,
castanetting on six-inch heels across the marble flags,
shuffling on rubber sandals across the marble flags,
out of Daimlers and Cadillacs,
Fiats and Delages.

Their followers are pot-bellies in bérets,
lean bellies in tweeds,

fierce snappers of cameras,
crouching,
leaning,
genuflecting,
before dividing up the last morsels of multitudinous hors
     d'oeuvres,
the final succulent flakes of tartine maison,
under the striped umbrellas that leave them too much in the
     sun,
too much out of the sun,
too much in the wind,
not enough in the gentle breeze . . .
until at last they stagger their plugged bodies,
pressed down and overflowing,
back on to the sagging cushions of Daimler and Cadillac,
Fiat and Delage . . .
but not before glancing at the pretty pictures in the inn,
the Matisses, the Braques, the Vlamincks, the Laurencins, the
     Utrillos . . .

"Really, you know! Vraiment, ma chère! Quite remarkable,
    no?"

O Piper, why do you have to blow sour notes?
Or is it the law that you cannot pick and choose,
that you can stop none from their running?

Mere bodies, you say.
Indeed? But what, then, of souls?

When the working light has yielded to orange,
and scarlet tinged with green,
making the great vault a flaming black opal;
the sleepy doves roucouling on the still warm tiles,
the big fire within no longer at work,
but glowing, inviting . . .
then come the souls,
one by one,
gathering,
seeking release,
their inner fire equally glowing, inviting;
in sweaters and sandals,
in slacks and scarves,
crowding the arched bar and the passageways,
grouping at either immense fireplace in the wood-panelled
    halls;
glasses on piano,
on benches,
on floor,
freeing the hands for emphasis,
for minimisation,
for deprecation,
for mere illustration;
the spate of words seeking to be undammed from solitary
    workshop,
from studio,
from cloistered bed-sitting-working-room,
within or without the fortress town.

See them come . . .
painters,
shaved,
bearded,
as to the finger nails clean,
unclean . . . what matters;
piped or cigaretted.
Their perfume is not Chanel,
but turps and linseed and caporal.
Their hunger is not satisfied through the stomach
from sardine to tartine;
but rather in putting food for others
on canvas,
paper,
glass,
wood,
carton,
pottery,
walls . . .
on any surface that will receive and retain their colored dream
of heaven,
of hell,
of mere earth,
of sex . . .
old school,
new school,
no school;
their own school,
distorted,
geometric,
romantic,
primitive,
post-surrealist . . .
who cares, if it has the spark that irritates, that urges?

See others come . . .
poets,

looking like poets,
not looking like poets,
young-old,
old-young,
male,
female,
both at once,
neither;
poets, alone in the empty crowded night,
alone with tortured intestines out of which is born, at last,
a verse,
a line,
a word . . .
the word . . .
born, or still-born,
born to be mashed to death with agonised pencil,
and, out of its unmourned grave,
tempting little harlots of words crying aloud to be taken.

Poets, chained by the leg in the enormous mansions of their
    imagery;
mountains, tremblingly and finally bringing forth verbal
    mouse,
satisfied only if mouse be alive,
be the distillation of a single drop of universal truth.
Poets,
round the fireplace,
with painter,
with woman,
with any other kind of artist,
at a pinch with any layman, any body,
as victim,
as target,
as mere pair of ears into which to unleash the new-born word-
    mouse;
watching hawk-eyed,
hawk-eared,
to see,

to hear,
to feel,
to smell,
if word-truth and color-truth be one,
be same,
even in their difference.

There come also musicians—
sports of the same litter—
since, to them,
word and color are but half-truth;
since, to them,
the final answer is sound:
that cannot be the half of anything,
but is . . .
like rain,
like sea,
like sun.

On the long keyboard of black and white,
of itself mute, unsentient,
their arduous fingers,
instantly obedient,
refined,
half godlike,
recreate the already living and created sound-truth,
touch burning sun,
dip into wet blue sea,
call down the gentle rain,
impregnate the four-walled universe
until you, who are no poet,
write unwritable poems in the ether as you hear;
until you, who are no painter,
see unpaintable paintings in the ether as you hear;
until you, who are no musician,
are consumed wholly by the fire of music as you hear.

In the great scheme of things,
these, all,

painters, poets, musicians,
may be nothing, count for nothing . . .
just gaily colored threads in the dark pattern,
lengths of polished copper to conduct the cosmic lightning
    when it strikes.
Yet are they odd lengths,
different,
obéissant appointed channels,
keyed to the snap and crackle when the current flows,
outrating and outlasting emperors;
but, current off, most needful of pity and of cosseting,
waiting,
useless,
driven,
sagging below the level of us all,
the Marthas,
whose humble lot it is to fetch, to carry, to feed, to comfort,
and, perhaps, with faint stirring, to know the pangs of envy.

And their women?
For what could they do, what be,
without women, whether for succor only, or for sex?
The woman in them,
integral, essential,
without which not,
cannot suffice.
They must kiss a lingering hand,
lingeringly;
read the understanding message behind soft eyes,
whether of familiar doting grandmother,
or, better, of sweet young thing,
unbruised,
but deliciously suspecting,
ready with rapturous eyes and wondrous ears,
all kitten-bodied and awaiting the stroking . . .
and giving by the mere act of receiving that which, miscalled
    homage,
is man's listening to his own echo.

Into the Inn of the Golden Dove gather these appointed ones,
negligent of the unimportant—
race, creed, patched-up frontiers—
speaking in many tongues which are all one;
pores open,
urgent,
simple in their complexity,
apostles in self-faith,
migratory brothers of the strutting doves,
sharing with gusto the heady spiritual nourishment,
group-created,
by themselves and for themselves;
yet egocentrically intent,
each one,
to split his individual atom of the working days,
until, refreshed and self-enkindled,
each must spread reluctant wings . . .

And you, fantastic Piper,
you sit basking in the knowledge of one proven fact:
that they will all come back to you,
and back again,
to dispense of their inner treasure,
and, thereby, add once more thereto.

ANTIBES

1. *I Was a Stranger: and You Fed Me*

Antibes and its Cap: one and inseparable;
separated, nevertheless,
by swelling acres of Royalty,
by glittering fringe of Hollywood.
Between,
the French . . .

Odd worlds, these three, in so short a mileage;
the first two impermanent as birds of Paradise upon a branch,
dropping golden feathers;
the third in permanence before ever Greeks and Saracens
   came
to put strange words into their mouths.

Our villa touched the fringe of Hollywood:
but, though we saw, we were not conquered;
while even to glimpse Royalty,

except by accident,
was to aspire too high.
But the French . . .

There came black morning
when American banks suspended payment,
when credit letter, cheques, became as nothing,
became as bits of torn up paper.
For money: loose change at the bottom of a pocket.
We were two strangers,
foreigners.
And then the French . . .

The landlord phoned:
"I send immediately a chasseur with some thousand-franc
   notes. When you need more, you tell me!"
The baker's wife shrugged:
"You come every day. Take all the bread you need. One must
   eat, no?"
The butcher produced a leg of lamb:
"Money? But I beg of you, do not occupy yourself of it!"
The wine merchant smiled in his beard:
"Eh bien, quoi! You pay me some day . . . One needs a
   good glass of wine to support a such blow! I send you a
   dozen bottles before noon."

Thus the French . . .
everyone,
everywhere.
And how much more than bread alone . . .

2. The Enchanted Villa

More than hands went to your building.
Every brick of you was an expression of giving,
a planned affection,
a selfless vision of days of happiness for others,
in this room and that,
as walls grew,
and floors were laid,
and furniture arranged with artistic eye,
and sun came shining into your finished windows
that looked across trees, rocks and sea
to the flowing swellings of the Estérel.

The pink wash you received held not stale aftertaint of profit.
You were not conceived to sell yourself to the hucksters in the
    marketplace.
You were a love-child,
born in the garden of Eden,

tucked lovingly into your bed of mimosa;
jonquils, roses and narcissus spread around your feet.

The sea sends up its tang to you.
The twinkling lights of Cannes are a necklace dangled before
    your eyes.
Old Antibes, from the end of the road, keeps grandmotherly
    watch over you.
The snow-covered Alps, from the lookout behind, link you to
    faint far Italy,
birthplace of the man who sired you.
Snug and warm, at your right side, lies your little friend, Juan-
    les-Pins.
And all the days of your life the sun has been your playmate.

The way to you is not easy,
nor short,
nor should it be.
Without struggle, the apples of Hesperides would have no
    worth.
Of this, we claimed some slight acquaintance,
with the serving of apprenticeship to expert killing,
to sight and smell of broken dead,
to the sucking mud of aftermath,
to the slow process of return to cleanliness.

Such schooling,
harsh then,
now normal,
you must have found sufficient;
for what you gave was not mere housing,
mere mute acceptance of passersby in momentary pause.
In this room and that,
in sun and rain,
by day, by night,
you gave the essence of what had gone to your building.
Your ambiance, in fullest meaning, was that of home:
minuscule kingdom,

wherein man and woman,
having found each other,
may grow to new meanings,
to heightened awareness,
to unsuspected depth;
may share and lay up secret spiritual treasure,
alert against tarnish,
jealous against interruption;
may put down roots that interlace,
giving and receiving nourishment throughout the years;
where children may scamper on unanxious feet,
owning and yet belonging,
giving and receiving,
themselves both root and flower,
themselves both echo and making echo,
themselves both answer and recurring question.

This you had known,
had been,
and now returned in lift and urgency.
You made words come freely to a hesitant pen,
add up to chapters,
become at last, triumphantly, a book.
You poured out color like strong wine,
so that venturing neophytes made proud horrific daubs of you
  on canvas.
You tempted a Saint Antony with delectable women and am-
  brosial food on the terrace at the garden's end.
You held out the quieter charm of friendly speech and welcoming smile
in neighboring shops when marketing for wine, for bread, for
  cheese.
You offered the caricaturist his fill in nearby Cannes,
there to crowd his sketchbook with a hundred types—
old satyrs with young girls;
old harridans with young boys;
beribboned Generals, never, in any war, with muddied boots;
women of Lesbos;

homos;
film actors acting without benefit of camera;
hard-working gigolos, worthy of their hire;
virgins who soon wouldn't be;
female stars whose twinkling had become synthetic;
starlets with playboys hitched to their luscious wagons . . .
for of all such is the kingdom of the Croisette.

You pointed to adventure,
whether in the winding alleys of sea-swept Antibes,
or on the winding roads that beckoned to the hill towns—
nests of Roman eagles,
perched precariously in loveliness,
each one an opal on green velvet,
backed up by jagged Alps;
each one as lonely from the other as planet from planet;
to be won to only after breath-taking hairpins
through burdened orange groves and blossoming mimosa,
straight cypresses and twisted olives.

And when, each evening,
the enriching variety of work and adventure was climaxed
by that final glimpse of heaven called "afterglow,"
splashing incredibly both mountain and sea,
you were there to come back to,
glowing in the last light,
restful,
sustaining,
inviting good talk after good food,
with new friends and old,
before the hearth where pine cones snapped and flamed
in punctuation and accompaniment.

Three times you drew us like a magnet;
three winters,
to work,
to play a little,
to feel,

to learn,
to store up,
perhaps, subconsciously, to grow.

Today, with another war between,
we have seen you rejuvenated,
new dressed in a fresh coat of pink,
in readiness again for such other lucky ones as may find their
    way to you.

May there be many who,
as we do,
will hold you in lasting gratitude and affection.

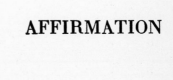

AFFIRMATION

Through all the land of France today
rings out the good folk-music of man's eternal faith in self;
music of sweat and urge,
of soil and heritage,
of purpose in full continuance.

There are today,
as there ever were,
Maids in Domrémy.
It was the spirit of the Maid that later said: "Ils ne passeront
    pas!"
and proved it;
her spirit that also said: "On les aura!"
and proved that;
her spirit again,
so very lately,
that flamed and would not die in the starving men,
and maids,
of the maquis.

Today another schoolboy, fifty years after me,
two wars after me,
may receive, and be moulded in his growing;
may learn, and unlearn, the same things that were then pre-
    sented to me:
the lasting things,
things unchanging,
and unchangeable either by victory or defeat . . .
so temporary, both,
as the old gargoyles well know who have watched both
during their coming,
their going,
and their coming again.

What need, then, now, of proclaiming Phoenix-risings from
    mere newspaper-ash?
In spirit and in mind,
in self-identity and self-expression,
in her present sowing and her future reaping,
in all that she has ever stood for
and in all that we have ever had to thank her for,
France is still France.